Scotland's Buses
in the 1960s

STEWART J. BROWN

based on the photographs of **HARRY HAY**

fawndoon

Scotland's Buses in the 1960s
First published by Fawndoon Books 2016

ISBN 978-0-9934831-0-3

Designed by Helen Swansbourne
Digital restoration by Peter Rowlands

Printed by Lavenham Press

Contents

PICTURE CREDITS
The bulk of the photographs
in this book, 230 out of 253,
were taken by Harry Hay.
The MacBrayne picture on
page 6 was taken by Robert
Grieves, and those of
Chieftain and Hutchison on
pages 116, 121 and 122 were
taken by Iain MacGregor. For
a small number of images
the original photographer is
not known; most have been
in the author's collection for
many years.

ABOVE: Sartorial elegance was clearly de rigueur among young bus
enthusiasts in the 1960s. Harry Hay (right) poses with his new Ford
Cortina on a 1966 trip, accompanied by Stewart Brown (centre) and
Gordon Ferguson.

FRONT COVER: Typical of new buses at the start of the 1960s is this
Aberdeen Corporation Daimler CVG6. 277 (ORG 277) was new in 1960
and had a 66-seat Metro-Cammell Orion body. The building in the
background is the city's Art Gallery.

BACK COVER: Guys made up just over 10 per cent of the predominantly
Leyland Central SMT fleet in 1960, with 45 single-deckers and 28
double-deckers. The latter included 16 Arab IIIs delivered in 1951–52
which had unusual Guy lowbridge bodies built on Park Royal frames.
H52 – with matching registration FVD 752 – heads out of Glasgow for
Wishaw. Central had started matching fleet and registration
numbers in 1948. The double-deck Arab IIIs were withdrawn in 1966.

OPPOSITE: Small-town bus operation in Scotland in the 1960s is nicely
captured in this scene in Kelso. On the right is a 1948 Albion Victor
FT39 with Scottish Aviation body, BKS 288, operated by Kyle Bros and
waiting to depart for Greatridge Hall. Buses with Roxburghshire KS
registrations were extremely rare. Alongside stands Scottish
Omnibuses AEC Regal III B398E (GSF 717) which had been new in 1949
with a half-cab Alexander body and was rebodied by Burlingham in
1954. The E suffix to the fleet number indicates that B398 was one of
the 27 buses based at SOL's depot in Kelso.

Introduction

"The past is a foreign country; they do things differently there." So wrote novelist L P Hartley. And how true it is.

In the 1960s most bus photographers were still using black-and-white film. A few were shooting colour slides, and an even smaller number, colour prints. The reason for the dominance of black-and-white was simple: cost. For most of the 1960s I was a teenager, using a Voigtlander folding camera which took eight photographs on a roll of 120 film. Film was expensive, and was used sparingly.

Harry Hay, whose photographs form the basis for this book, was a few years older than me, was working (I was still at school at the start of the decade), and could afford to spend more on film. His choice of colour negative rather than colour transparency was a simple one. He argued that you could look at colour prints at any time, where with colour slides you needed a screen, a projector and a darkened room to view them properly. He held that view until the late 1960s when he switched from a roll film camera to 35mm, and at the same time changed from taking prints to taking slides. Bear in mind the simplicity of 1960s roll-film cameras – no zoom lens, no auto focus, no integrated exposure meter, and the need after each exposure to use a knurled knob somewhere on the camera body to wind on the film, which was a strip about 30 inches long and 2½ inches wide. Like most photographers of the time Harry was a pretty good judge of the light and could set the exposure without using a light meter. The one noticeable downside of some of the negatives is limited depth of field – the bus can be sharp, but the background often isn't. Harry's rolls of exposed 120 Kodak Safety Film – that's how it is described on the negatives – were sent to London for processing by photographic specialist

▲ It's 1962, and Glasgow Corporation Leyland Titan PD2/24 L332 (SGD 334) heads east along Argyle Street on service 18 to Burnside, introduced in June 1961 to replace a tram route which had used the same number – the only time that a replacement bus service retained the number of the withdrawn tram service. Although it looks like an Alexander body, this Titan was actually bodied by the Corporation in its Coplawhill workshops. Corporation-built bodies on PD2s used a different style of glazing from those produced by Alexander. Ladders in front of the shop on the extreme right suggest Carter Tiling Edinburgh was working on the fascia. Mounts to hold the ladders can be seen on the roof of the Austin J2 van. The Singer Gazelle estate car was a rare vehicle.

Wallace Heaton. There were no one-hour film processors in the 1960s.

When I met Harry, in 1962, he was an electrician and living in Helensburgh, but he soon gave that career up, taking a job as a bus driver with his local company, Garelochhead Coach Services, later becoming an inspector. Among the other companies he worked for were Wallace Arnold, as a tour driver, and Western SMT, as a driver and later an inspector. He and a colleague left Western in 1990 to set up their own company, Shuttle Buses, based in Kilwinning. Sadly Harry didn't live to see it develop. He died in 1991, aged 49. A fair number of the pictures in this book were taken on trips which Harry and I made together and I make cameo appearances in three of them. Equally, Harry occasionally appears in the black-and-white pictures I was taking on these same trips.

I inherited his negative collection – a treasure trove of 1960s Scottish buses – which provided the impetus for this book. Although the project grew as I worked on it, most of the colour illustrations in the pages which follow are Harry's, 230 out of 251, and only a few have appeared in print before. One of the things he came to realise in taking colour photographs was that good light made a huge difference to the results. So, while he did take photographs on dull and rainy days – cynics might say he had little choice, living in Scotland – where possible he waited for the sun to come out. That produced a lot of stunning images, and this volume may help to perpetuate the myth that the summers were always better in days gone by…

A measure of the change which has taken place in the last half century is that every single bus and coach illustrated in these pages is British-built.

One challenge in selecting images for this book was striking a balance between those vehicles which typify the period, and the unusual one-offs which seemed much more interesting and which dedicated enthusiasts such as Harry and I spent many happy hours tracking down. Anyway, in *Scotland's Buses in the 1960s* I have tried to capture something of the spirit of the country's bus and coach operators in that decade. I hope you enjoy the result.

My thanks to three good friends who have helped ensure the quality of this book, designer Helen Swansbourne, Peter Rowlands who worked his Photoshop magic on scans of 50-year-old negatives, and Gavin Booth, who kindly read the proofs.

Stewart J. Brown
Hebden Bridge, 2016

The big picture: 1960s Scotland

cotland's four biggest cities, Glasgow, Edinburgh, Aberdeen and Dundee, were each served by municipal buses, with Glasgow also running trams (until 1962), trolleybuses (until 1967) and a 6½-mile underground railway. Officially this was the Underground, but colloquially it was the Subway. Between them, the four municipals ran 2,600 buses. Elsewhere the Scottish Bus Group (SBG) was the main operator. At the start of the decade it operated almost 4,000 buses and coaches which carried 767 million passengers. The buses were run

▲ MacBrayne's buses were a colourful part of the Highland transport scene. Rest and be Thankful was the summit of the A83 road between Arrochar and Inveraray. Trunk services to and from Glasgow connected there with a local service which ran to Lochgoilhead and Carrick Castle. Two Duple-bodied AEC Reliances pause on northbound services from Glasgow, while 1965 Bedford VAS1 146 (EGA 834C) is on the Carrick Castle route, with its blind still set for Top of Rest, an enigmatic destination for those who didn't know its meaning. The 29-seat Duple Midland body on the Bedford has glazed cove panels.

▼ At the start of the 1960s there were just two Leyland Atlanteans in Scotland. The first of these was Glasgow Corporation LA1 (FYS 998) and it featured in this Leyland advert from the January 1962 edition of leading trade magazine *Bus & Coach*, announcing the Corporation's order for 150. The blurb claimed that the order had been placed as a result of "the many advantages derived from the Atlantean's large seating capacity, its good acceleration and fuel consumption, together with passengers' praise of the low one-step entrance and of the superior riding qualities which result from the excellent weight distribution". It was photographed at Govan Cross terminus with shipyard cranes dominating the skyline. No doubt the boarding passengers were preparing to engage in serious discussion about the riding qualities of rear-engined buses, a hot topic of conversation in Govan in 1962.

▲ In 1961 Alexander was split into three new companies. There were a few places where it was possible to see vehicles of all three Alexander companies together – most noticeably Perth and, after the Tay Bridge opened in 1966, Dundee. It also happened in Glasgow, as seen here, regularly in the summer but also once a day right through the year, when a Northern bus arrived in the city on service 19 from Dundee which was operated jointly with Midland. Here Northern NAC156 (NMS 367) awaits its return home, at one o'clock, flanked by buses from Fife and Midland. The Fife bus is a Tiger Cub, which was lower-built than the Reliances alongside. Fife's FPD227 (RMS 716) has arrived on the limited-stop Saturday service 100 from St Andrews. Midland Reliance MAC182 (OMS 291) is on one of the two routes between Glasgow and Dunfermline which were operated jointly with Fife.

▼ After LA1 all of Glasgow's 1960s Atlanteans had this style of Alexander body. This postcard, produced for the city's Transport Museum, shows LA422 (PYS 950G) posed outside the Art Gallery at Kelvingrove. The original caption records that it was the Corporation's first one-man double-decker. Fitting a second door reduced its seating capacity from 78 to 75. Glasgow's buses in the 1960s did not look this smart for long.

GLASGOW SAYS "BIG BUSES ARE BETTER" – and orders 150 ATLANTEANS

THE **Leyland** ATLANTEAN
The Bus with the BIG future

LEYLAND MOTORS LTD

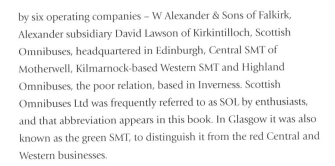

by six operating companies – W Alexander & Sons of Falkirk, Alexander subsidiary David Lawson of Kirkintilloch, Scottish Omnibuses, headquartered in Edinburgh, Central SMT of Motherwell, Kilmarnock-based Western SMT and Highland Omnibuses, the poor relation, based in Inverness. Scottish Omnibuses Ltd was frequently referred to as SOL by enthusiasts, and that abbreviation appears in this book. In Glasgow it was also known as the green SMT, to distinguish it from the red Central and Western businesses.

The Alexander Y-type was a significant model in Scotland. It was unveiled in 1961 and by 1969 there would be some 850 in operation, most of them with SBG. Alexander Midland was the only SBG company to take Leyland Tiger Cubs with Y-type bodies, building up a fleet of 31 in 1963–64. When new they were used as front-line coaches, as illustrated by MPD269 (AMS 300B) in Melrose on a tour from Glasgow to the Scott Country.

Buses were smaller and lighter half a century ago, and in 1960 SBG reported the average fuel consumption of its fleet as 10.47mpg for double-deckers, 13.11mpg for single-deckers, and 9.24mpg for petrol-engined coaches, which at this time were relatively small numbers of Bedfords and Commers.

Alexander alone ran around 2,000 vehicles in three operating areas, Southern, Fife and Northern. In 1961 these were separated as three distinct business – W Alexander & Sons (Midland), W Alexander & Sons (Fife) and W Alexander & Sons (Northern). The Lawson business, which ran 89 buses and coaches, was absorbed by Alexander Midland.

While SBG was primarily a bus operator, all of its subsidiaries ran coaches, and day excursions were operated in the summer months from most towns of any significance.

There were a number of substantial independent bus operators, particularly in Ayrshire (A1, AA, Clyde Coast) and the Paisley area (Cunningham's, Graham's, McGill's, Paton and Smith). In Lanarkshire three of the biggest independents – Chieftain of Hamilton, Baxter of Airdrie and Carmichael of Glenboig – were taken over by SBG in the 1960s, but others survived, the biggest being Hutchison of Overtown. The three major independents serving Aberdeen – Burnett, Strachan, and Simpson – were bought by Alexander Northern during the decade.

There was one other significant bus operator, David MacBrayne, serving parts of the west coast and many of the islands. MacBrayne also ran coach tours, operated steamers throughout the Western Isles, and had a large fleet of lorries. MacBrayne was an unusual business, owned equally by the state and by Coast Lines. That changed in 1969 when it became a wholly-owned subsidiary of the Scottish Transport Group, the new holding company for SBG. STG initially said that the MacBrayne bus operation would continue as a separate subsidiary, probably based in Inverness, but that was not to be and its bus operations would be absorbed by existing SBG businesses – primarily Highland Omnibuses – in the early 1970s.

All advertised bus and coach services on which fares were charged required a Road Service Licence, issued by the Traffic Commissioner. For scheduled services the licence specified the precise route, the timetable and the fares. For coach tours it specified pick-up points, destinations and fares, and could also put a limit on the number of coaches to be used or on the period of operation. Any changes to the licence required the approval of the

Traffic Commissioner, and applications to make changes often attracted objections from other operators or from British Railways.

Parcel and newspaper deliveries were an important part of SBG's business, particularly in rural areas. Western SMT, for example, had parcel agents in 72 towns and villages, including the delightful-sounding Beeswing. At its busiest bus stations SBG employed parcel boys. That term sounded less insulting in the 1960s than it does now, when they would probably be called package service operatives and would require an appropriate SVQ, the Scottish Vocational Qualification. The parcel boys were generally too young to be employed as conductors, and part of their job was to ensure that

goods in the parcels office were delivered to the correct buses for onward delivery.

Pick any decade and you'll find change taking place, much of which, when you're a teenager, you don't readily appreciate or fully understand. But consider some of the things which happened in Scotland in the 1960s. In 1960 there were just two rear-engined double-deckers in service. These were Glasgow Corporation's pioneering Atlantean, LA1, and a second Atlantean, XVA 444, running with Chieftain of Hamilton. By 1969 there were over 1,000 rear-engined double-deckers in Scotland – half of them Atlanteans in Glasgow. Early

▼ The most popular coach with small operators in the early 1960s was the Duple-bodied Bedford. Sales in Scotland were handled by SMT Sales & Service which had a proper showroom for coaches at its premises in Finnieston, Glasgow. The only new coach bought by Smith of Grantown-on-Spey was a Bedford SB5 with Duple Bella Vega body, purchased in 1964. 20 (MSO 579) was the most modern vehicle in the fleet when the Smith business was purchased by Highland Omnibuses in 1966. SO was a Morayshire registration; the number of Morayshire-registered buses in service in Scotland in the 1960s could be counted on the fingers of one hand. Period touches are a Bedford Drivers Club badge, the small blue disc visible to the right of the Bedford badge, and a small flower display in the centre of the windscreen.

operating experience of rear-engined buses wasn't always good, and at the end of the decade SBG was complaining that their running costs were 50 per cent higher than for older types of double-decker.

Half-cab single-deckers were still commonplace in 1960 – there were 900 in SBG service alone – but they slowly disappeared and by 1969 there were around 100 survivors with SBG, and only a handful with independents. The biggest fleet of half-cab single-deckers at the end of the decade was at Alexander Northern, which still had 60 in service, all of them the best part of 20 years old.

In 1960 there were very few one-man-operated buses, and these were mainly in deep rural areas. By 1969 one-man-operation was becoming widespread, and was being introduced on double-deckers, with both Edinburgh and Glasgow adding dual-door one-man-operated Atlanteans to their fleets. The logic was that a second exit cut waiting time at bus stops, but the gain was often marginal and Glasgow would abandon the two-door

▲ The lowbridge Leyland Titan PD3 was a bus which could be found in most parts of Scotland, from Ayr in the south-west to Peterhead in the north-east. There were 325 of them, although it seemed like more, and all were 67-seaters. Most had Alexander bodies, as seen on Midland MRB270 (SWG 626) pulling out of Falkirk bus station with the simplified style of fleetname adopted in 1968. The fleetname might have been simplified, but the livery was still fully lined out, a practice which would be abandoned in the 1970s.

layout in the mid 1970s. And, of course, the buses were one *man* operated, although in 1968 Glasgow Corporation general manager E R L Fitzpayne noted: "There is nothing to stop women driving single-manned buses. The modern bus is as easily handled by a woman as a man." I can't imagine that sentiment went down well in the macho world which was 1960s Glasgow. Drivers of one-man buses in Glasgow were paid an extra 25 per cent to compensate for the additional work of collecting fares. At SBG the rate was a less generous 15 per cent. At terminal points where a reversing manoeuvre was needed, in theory under the watchful eye of the conductor, routes were often revised so that one-man buses didn't have to reverse. This change, of course, required the Traffic Commissioner's approval.

Scotland largely avoided the troublesome rear-engined single-deckers which were often used to introduce one-man-operation in towns and cities south of the border. Glasgow bought 16 Leyland Panthers, but these were short-lived. They were the only new Panthers for a Scottish operator. Aberdeen took 25 AEC Swifts towards the end of the 1960s (and another 12 in 1970–71) after having bought a dozen Leyland Tiger Cubs with unusual two-door Alexander Y-type bodies in 1966–67. Dundee tried high-capacity AEC Reliances, but in a city where there was a long history of trade union activism, these buses lay idle for over a year before entering service in 1966. They were followed by rear-engined Swifts in 1968.

Edinburgh experimented with a high-capacity single-decker, too, fleet number 101. This was a 36ft-long Leyland Leopard with one of the first Alexander Y-type bodies, and it was configured with just 33 seats, a wide rear entrance and two exits, one in mid wheelbase and the other at the front. But this was not a one-man bus; boarding passengers paid their fares to a seated conductor. The bus was inspired by continental European practice and was not a success. In 1969 101 had its rear and centre doors removed, was upseated to 45, and was then allocated to the operator's coach fleet. It would later be bought for preservation and impressively restored to its original condition.

The 24-hour clock appeared for the first time in Scottish bus timetables in 1965, when it was adopted as standard by SBG. At the same time the layout of the timetables was improved, making them much easier to use. There was a timetable book for each SBG subsidiary, and for most of the decade the price was 4d.

There were no motorways in Scotland in 1960. By 1969 parts of the M8 and M74 were open – but completion of the M74 from Glasgow to the English border would take another 42 years, while the M8 is still incomplete between Glasgow and Edinburgh. Motorways would transform long-distance coach travel, but not in 1960s Scotland. What did bring change were new bridges across the estuaries of two of Scotland's major rivers. The

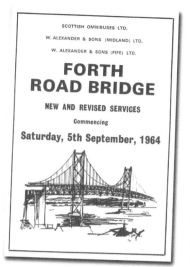

SCOTTISH OMNIBUSES LTD.

W. ALEXANDER & SONS (MIDLAND) LTD.

W. ALEXANDER & SONS (FIFE) LTD.

FORTH ROAD BRIDGE

NEW AND REVISED SERVICES

Commencing

Saturday, 5th September, 1964

Forth Road Bridge opened in 1964, providing a direct link between Fife and Edinburgh. It was at the time the longest suspension bridge in Europe, and the fourth-longest in the world with a main span of 3,298ft and a total length of 8,242ft. Then the Tay Road Bridge, connecting Fife with Dundee city centre, opened in 1966. Its total length was 7,382ft. The opening of both bridges saw the withdrawal of long-established ferry services and the introduction of new cross-river bus services.

In Glasgow, a tunnel under the Clyde was opened in 1963. Both Glasgow Corporation and Western SMT routed services through it, but it did not have any major long-term impact on the bus route network. Paton of Renfrew also applied for a licence to run through the tunnel but then withdrew the application. Work was underway on a bridge across the Clyde to replace a ferry at Erskine at the end of the decade, but it would not open until 1971. A new motorway link across the Clyde in Glasgow, the M8 Kingston Bridge, opened in 1970.

The Beeching plan, *The Reshaping of British Railways*, was published in 1963 and it proposed the closure of many lines and stations in Scotland. These were, mostly, little-used routes, although had the Beeching plan been implemented in its entirety there would have been no rail services north or west of Inverness. Indeed, in 1964 both Highland Omnibuses and MacBrayne applied for licences to run services from Inverness to Kyle of Lochalsh, in anticipation of that line's closure. The line was reprieved. The Beeching cuts saw some 700 Scottish stations being closed in the 1960s, but the closures had no significant impact on bus services which indicates how few passengers those stations were catering for. A few rail-replacement bus routes were introduced, but were usually short-lived.

In September 1968 the Labour government introduced a grant of 25 per cent towards the cost to operators of buying new buses, provided they were suitable for one-man operation. This would have a significant influence on fleet replacement, but not until the 1970s.

At various times throughout the decade there were discussions about SBG taking over the bus operations of Glasgow Corporation, but these came to naught. ∎

Principal SBG depots

Thurso

Wick

Tain

Buckie
Rosehearty
Elgin
Macduff
Dingwall
Peterhead
Inverness
Huntly
Fyvie

Aberdeen

Stonehaven

Pitlochry
Montrose
Forfar
Blairgowrie
Arbroath

Dundee

Oban
Crieff
Perth
Newburgh
St Andrews
Cupar
Anstruther
Aberhill

Kelty
Lochgelly
Stirling
Alloa
Cowdenbeath
Kirkcaldy
Balfron
Bannockburn
Dunfermline
Kilsyth
Grangemouth
Old Kilpatrick
Milngavie
Kirkintilloch
Falkirk
Linlithgow
Edinburgh
Dunbar
Greenock
Stepps
Cumbernauld
Broxburn
Musselburgh
Inchinnan
Bailleston
Airdrie
Bathgate
Dalkeith
Johnstone
Hamilton
Motherwell
Rothesay
Newton Mearns
Wishaw
Berwick
East Kilbride
Carluke
Peebles
Ardrossan
Galashiels
Kilmarnock
Kelso
Ayr
Cumnock
Hawick

Dumfries

The Scottish Bus Group's services covered most of the country, and this is clearly seen in the distribution of its main depots, located in the 74 towns listed below. There were in addition outstations in a number of other places. The sizes of the depots varied considerably from the huge Eastern Scottish premises in New Street, Edinburgh, with 273 buses and coaches, down to tiny rural depots, such as those operated by Northern in Fyvie and Huntly with just six buses each.

Depot codes are shown where they were routinely displayed on the vehicles. Central did not use depot codes at all. Highland did so for a short time, but the practice died out in the early 1960s.

Town	Operator	Depot code	1966 vehicle allocation
Aberdeen	Northern	A	119
Aberhill	Fife	AL	71
Airdrie Clarkston	Eastern	H	82
Airdrie Victoria	Eastern	V	50
Alloa	Midland	A	60
Anstruther	Fife	A	26
Arbroath	Northern	AH	20
Ardrossan	Western	N	49
Ayr	Western	A	133
Baillieston	Eastern	C	82
Balfron	Midland	B	28
Bannockburn	Midland	BN	57
Bathgate	Eastern	B	99
Berwick	Eastern	J	15
Blairgowrie	Northern	B	17
Broxburn	Eastern	I	41
Buckie	Northern	B	10
Carluke	Central	-	41
Cowdenbeath	Fife	C	47
Crieff	Midland	C	27
Cumbernauld	Midland	CD	n/a (opened 1968)
Cumnock	Western	C	52
Cupar	Fife	CR	30
Dalkeith	Eastern	G	56
Dingwall	Highland	D	26
Dumfries	Western	D	147
Dunbar	Eastern	S	14
Dundee	Northern	D	65
Dunfermline	Fife	D	125
East Kilbride	Central	-	98
Edinburgh	Eastern	A	273
Elgin	Northern	E	55
Falkirk (Larbert)	Midland	L	119
Forfar	Northern	FR	21
Fyvie	Northern	F	6
Galashiels	Eastern	D	30
Grangemouth	Midland	G	91

Town	Operator	Depot code	1966 vehicle allocation
Greenock	Western	G	150
Hamilton	Central	-	111
Hawick	Eastern	L	15
Huntly	Northern	H	6
Inchinnan	Western	I	83
Inverness	Highland	I	60
Johnstone	Western	J	154
Kelso	Eastern	E	27
Kelty	Fife	KY	43
Kilmarnock	Western	K	147
Kilsyth	Midland	K	61
Kirkcaldy	Fife	K	124
Kirkintilloch	Midland	KH	87
Linlithgow	Eastern	F	41
Lochgelly	Fife	LY	30
Macduff	Northern	MF	22
Milngavie	Midland	M	120
Motherwell	Central	-	161
Montrose	Northern	M	21
Musselburgh	Eastern	W	42
Newburgh	Fife	N	13
Newton Mearns	Western	M	94
Oban	Midland	ON	16
Old Kilpatrick	Central	-	121
Peebles	Eastern	K	11
Perth	Midland	P	81
Peterhead	Northern	P	26
Pitlochry	Midland	PY	11
Rosehearty	Northern	R	16
Rothesay	Western	R	28
St Andrews	Fife	StA	12
Stepps	Midland	SS	117
Stirling	Midland	S	84
Stonehaven	Northern	S	26
Tain	Highland	-	6
Thurso/Wick	Highland	C	63
Wishaw	Central	-	81

Glasgow: a city in decline

Glasgow was Scotland's biggest city in the 1960s, home to around 1.1 million people, roughly 20 per cent of the country's population. At the start of the decade it was served mainly by Glasgow Corporation Transport's fleet of buses, trolleybuses and trams. As recently as 1956 trams had outnumbered buses in the GCT fleet, but the trams were on the way out. By 1960 the Corporation was running almost 1,500 buses and trolleybuses, but just 200 trams. The bus fleet peaked at just under 1,550 in the middle of the decade (including 136 trolleybuses), but by 1969 was down to 1,300 – and the trolleybuses had gone. This reduction in the fleet size reflected a declining population, growing car

▲ Most of the Glasgow Corporation fleet in 1960 was in the traditional and attractive livery of orange, green and cream as seen on this 1959 Daimler CVG6 with 61-seat Alexander body and Manchester-style grille. D228 (SGD 211) is outside Queen's Park on the south side of the city and was one of 50 broadly similar Daimlers which were being delivered as the livery was being revised; later vehicles in this order were in the simplified scheme of yellow and green separated by a cream band above the lower deck windows, introduced in the summer of 1959 to facilitate spray painting. The last few motorbuses in the livery shown here were repainted in 1965. The passing van is a Thames 400E, the predecessor of the Ford Transit.

ownership and the use of 78-seat Leyland Atlanteans to replace early postwar 56-seat buses. In adopting the Atlantean Glasgow's aim was to use fewer bigger buses to provide broadly the same level of service in terms of capacity, if not frequency. But public transport use was in rapid decline, and GCT's passenger numbers fell dramatically, by 40 per cent from 500 million in 1960 to just over 300 million in 1969. The city's population fell by around 20 per cent over the same period.

In Glasgow's first wave of postwar bus buying between 1947 and 1953 – what might be called the exposed-radiator phase – the Corporation bought 515 new diesel buses and most of these were still in service at the start of the 1960s. These were mainly AEC

▲ When it was posted in September 1963 by an American holidaymaker to friends in Albany, New York, this delightful hand-tinted postcard of Jamaica Bridge was surely already old-fashioned, thanks to advances in colour photography and printing which facilitated the production of real colour postcards. The Leyland Titan nearest the camera is Glasgow's L268 (SGD 270) on the 38A to Clarkston. In reality the Austin FX4 taxis would have been black. There are still tram tracks on the bridge, but no trams in sight. The postcard's writer noted of his hotel room: "Chilly, but I see I have an electric heater that you put a shilling in!" The metal bridge on the left carries the tracks to Central Station.

◀ This is the cover of the brochure for what would be the final season for Lawson's Land Cruises, 1961. From 1962 Lawson's coach holidays would be incorporated in the Midland tour programme. The coach is one of six 37-seat Alexander-bodied AEC Reliances delivered to Lawson in 1960, and photographed outside The Old Albion Inn at Crantock in Cornwall. They were the last new vehicles for the company.

Regent IIIs (265), Albion Venturers (138) and Daimler CVD6s (108). Bodywork for these buses came from a variety of sources and made for an interesting fleet – Alexander, Brockhouse, Croft, Crossley, Mann Egerton, Metro-Cammell, Northern Coachbuilders, Roberts, Scottish Aviation, Weymann and the Corporation's own Larkfield bus works.

But standardisation was taking hold. In the mid 1950s GCT took delivery of 149 AEC Regent Vs, Daimler CVG6s and Leyland Titan PD2s with identical 60-seat bodies built by Weymann and Alexander. Then from 1957 the standard became the Daimler CVG6 and Leyland Titan PD2 with 61-seat Alexander bodywork or, on some of the PD2s, Alexander-style bodywork built in Coplawhill workshops. Odd modern types in the 1960 fleet were the Corporation's first 30ft-long motorbus, D217, a Daimler CD650-30 which had been an exhibit at the 1957 Scottish Motor Show; LA1, Scotland's first rear-engined double-decker, which had entered service in December 1958 after being exhibited at the Commercial Motor Show in London in September; and the last new Daimler-engined buses for

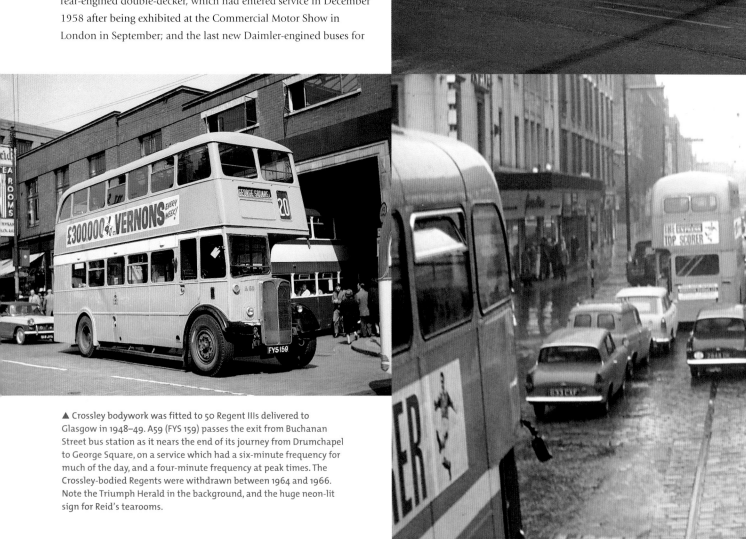

▲ Crossley bodywork was fitted to 50 Regent IIIs delivered to Glasgow in 1948–49. A59 (FYS 159) passes the exit from Buchanan Street bus station as it nears the end of its journey from Drumchapel to George Square, on a service which had a six-minute frequency for much of the day, and a four-minute frequency at peak times. The Crossley-bodied Regents were withdrawn between 1964 and 1966. Note the Triumph Herald in the background, and the huge neon-lit sign for Reid's tearooms.

◄ Easily the biggest supplier of new buses to Glasgow Corporation in the early postwar years was AEC, which provided 265 Regent IIIs between 1948 and 1952. There were 195 with this style of 56-seat body built by both Metro-Cammell and Weymann. A252 (FYS 435) of 1951 is seen at Govan Cross, which in the 1960s was an area of shipyards and densely-populated tenements. Operation of Regent IIIs ended in 1967. Standfast was a brand of whisky. In the days before the widespread use of credit cards the Jago carpet and furniture shop advertises "Cash or easiest terms". The River Clyde flows behind the tenements to the right of the bus.

▲ Glasgow Corporation was the only operator to order double-deck bodies from Scottish Aviation of Prestwick. It took 20 – ten to rebody prewar AEC Regents, and five each on new Albion Venturer and Daimler CVD6 chassis. D64 (FYS 492) is a CVD6, seen in the northern suburb of Milton, clearly Paradise Lost. New in 1950, it was withdrawn in 1965. The odd-looking destination display was the result of a cost-saving exercise; originally intermediate points on the route were displayed in the panel below the final destination. The 1959 livery initially featured yellow front wings as seen here, but from around 1963 these were painted black – harder wearing but less attractive.

The granite cobbles glisten in Argyle Street, just west of Central Station, with 1938 64-seat Coronation tram 1212 heading east to Auchenshuggle on route 9 from Dalmuir West, a distance of 11 miles. The Corporation Leyland Titan ahead of the maroon Ford Anglia was one of a small number which did not have the band of cream relief between the yellow and green.

Scotland, five CVD6s which entered service towards the end of 1959.

Single-deckers played but a small part in Glasgow's operations, usually being found on suburban services where there were low bridges, notably around the Hillington Industrial Estate in the west, and on a route which passed under the railway at Carntyne in the east. Of the 1,300 motorbuses in the 1960 fleet, fewer than 70 were single-deckers – two-door Daimler CVD6s and Leyland Worldmasters.

The trolleybus network, started in 1949, reached its peak at the end of 1958 with just over 43 route miles operated by 194 trolleybuses. The network was intact in 1960 but was gradually dismantled between 1962 and 1967, when the last trolleybus ran on 27 May. The oldest vehicles were 64 high-capacity three-axle BUTs and Daimlers with 70-seat London-style Metro-Cammell bodies. These were in the 1960s Scotland's heaviest buses, weighing

▼ Glasgow's first trolleybuses were 65 three-axle Metro-Cammell-bodied 70-seaters broadly similar to vehicles being supplied to London Transport. There were 35 BUTs and 30 Daimlers, and they entered service in 1949–50. Daimler CTM6 TD13 (FYS 747) heads south on Saltmarket on its way from Royston Road to Polmadie. This livery layout was applied only to trolleybuses, with the roof being green rather than cream to help hide carbon deposits from the trolley heads. From 1959 those trolleybuses that were repainted received the same yellow and green livery as the motor bus fleet. Tern, which features on the billboard on the right, was a brand of shirt.

9tons 19cwt 3qr unladen. Then came 20 two-axle Sunbeam F4s and finally 90 handsome two-axle 71-seat BUT 9613Ts bodied by Crossley. The youngest of these vehicles were just eight years old when the system closed.

The small single-deck trolleybus fleet included the first buses over 30ft in length to operate in Britain. These were ten 1958 BUTs with 34ft 6in-long 50-seat Burlingham bodies which were used exclusively on service 108. This replaced south-side suburban tram route 12 between Mount Florida and Paisley Road Toll, a route which did not pass through the city centre. They were operated under dispensation from the Ministry of Transport; buses over 30ft in length did not become legal in Britain until 1961 when the limit was raised to 36ft. The long BUTs were withdrawn in 1967 and the route was converted to double-deck motorbuses.

At the start of the 1960s Glasgow was in the throes of a major fleet renewal, taking delivery of almost 400 buses in just three years, partly to replace the last trams, but also for the routine replacement of time-expired buses. It started by buying 229 30ft-long forward-entrance 72-seat AEC Regent Vs and Leyland Titan PD3s, before switching to the Leyland Atlantean with a new and attractive style of Alexander body. This was 30ft 8in long, taking advantage of the 1961 relaxation of the length limits for PSVs, with the extra eight inches allowing the use of curved windscreens and marking a distinct break away from the boxy look of early Atlanteans. The first of these arrived in 1962, and the Alexander-bodied Atlantean became the standard Corporation bus. The only other types

▲ Glasgow's first buses with new-look fronts entered service in 1955, apart from a solitary Daimler which had been an exhibit at the 1954 Commercial Motor Show. These were a mixture of AEC Regent Vs, Daimler CVG6s and Leyland Titan PD2s, all with this style of 60-seat bodywork built by Weymann, or by Alexander using Weymann frames. There were 75 AECs, 49 Daimlers and 25 Leylands. The AECs were in some respects CVG6 clones (not that the word clone was in common circulation in the 1950s) with Gardner 6LW engines and pre-selector gearboxes. Their service lives varied from 11 to 15 years. Regent A318 (FYS 624) heads out of the city on Parliamentary Road, while CVG6 D96 (FYS 551) crosses Jamaica Bridge on its way to Newlands. The pressed metal grille on the AEC was of a style specified only by the Glasgow, Aberdeen and Liverpool municipal fleets. It was fitted to all of Glasgow's Regent Vs, and to five for Aberdeen. The Birmingham-style grille on the Daimler has been modified by Glasgow, with horizontal slats above the registration number.

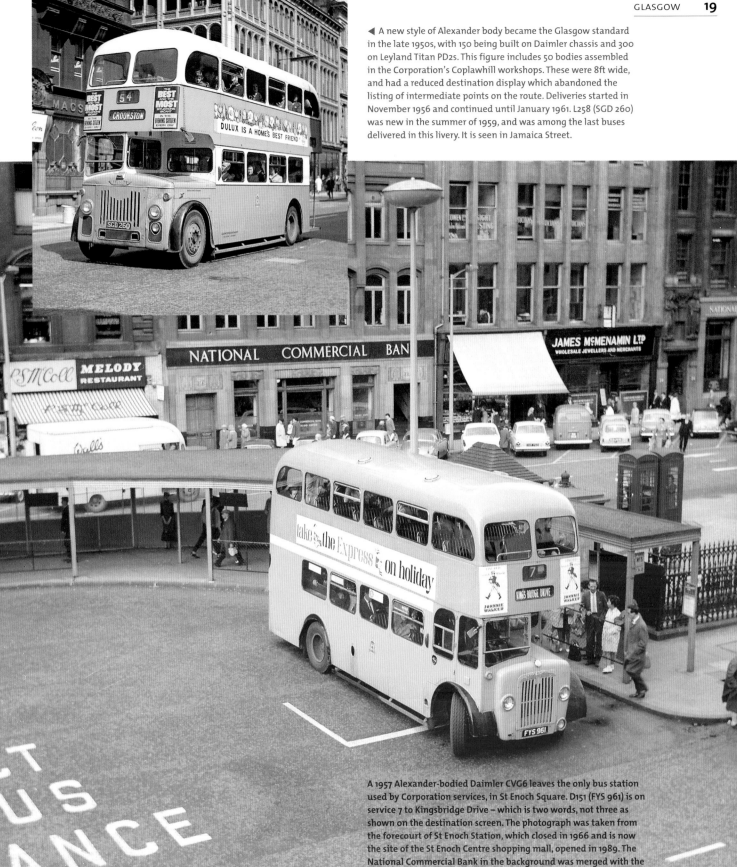

◀ A new style of Alexander body became the Glasgow standard in the late 1950s, with 150 being built on Daimler chassis and 300 on Leyland Titan PD2s. This figure includes 50 bodies assembled in the Corporation's Coplawhill workshops. These were 8ft wide, and had a reduced destination display which abandoned the listing of intermediate points on the route. Deliveries started in November 1956 and continued until January 1961. L258 (SGD 260) was new in the summer of 1959, and was among the last buses delivered in this livery. It is seen in Jamaica Street.

A 1957 Alexander-bodied Daimler CVG6 leaves the only bus station used by Corporation services, in St Enoch Square. D151 (FYS 961) is on service 7 to Kingsbridge Drive – which is two words, not three as shown on the destination screen. The photograph was taken from the forecourt of St Enoch Station, which closed in 1966 and is now the site of the St Enoch Centre shopping mall, opened in 1989. The National Commercial Bank in the background was merged with the Royal Bank of Scotland in 1969.

Trolleybuses operated in Glasgow from 1949 to 1967. The most numerous type was the two-axle 30ft-long BUT 9613T with attractive 71-seat Crossley bodywork, 90 of which entered service in 1957-58. Many were withdrawn and sold for scrap after just six years' service as the system was cut back. TB60 (FYS 821) loads at Govan Cross on the city's longest trolleybus route, the 106 which ran from Bellahouston to Millerston, a distance of almost ten miles. The destination screens on trolleybuses were green rather than black, and the route numbers were in a separate series from 101 to 108.

◀ For tramway replacement Glasgow placed large orders for high-capacity forward-entrance buses. These were 30ft-long 72-seaters, 89 Regent Vs and 140 PD3s. The bodies were by Alexander or, on 25 of the Titans, were built by the Corporation using Alexander parts. They were delivered between the summer of 1960 and the autumn of 1962. The Titans carried Albion badges, inset in the Leyland shield. L453 (SGD 455) passes the North British Hotel in George Square on route 58 to Dalmarnock, introduced as a tram replacement service in 1960. The hotel survives, and is now the Millennium.

▶ Single-deckers played a small part in Glasgow's operations, and at the start of the 1960s there were just 90 in the fleet – 38 Daimler CVD6s, 30 Leyland Worldmasters, one Daimler Freeline and 21 BUT trolleybuses. Most of the Worldmasters were delivered in 1956-57, and had 40-seat dual-door bodies built by the Corporation using Weymann frames. All had their centre doors removed between 1960 and 1963, and were up-seated to 44. They were normally to be found on suburban routes with low bridges, including the 30 which operated between Carmyle and North Carntyne, as seen here with LS25 (FYS 696). The route passed under a 12ft-high railway bridge in Carntyne.

ILLUSTRATED GUIDE TO GLASGOW

WHAT TO SEE · WHERE TO SEE
GLASGOW'S PLACES OF INTEREST
FULLY ILLUSTRATED :: 2/6 NET

30 CARMYLE to NORTH CARNTYNE

◀ Ten of the BUT single-deckers operated by Glasgow were noteworthy in being 34ft 6in long at a time when the legal limit was 30ft. They were allocated to suburban service 108, running under dispensation from the Ministry of Transport. New in 1958, they had 50-seat bodies by Burlingham. TBS14 (FYS 989) is seen at the Mount Florida terminus, ready to leave for Paisley Road Toll.

delivered between 1962 and 1969 were a solitary Daimler Fleetline, and 16 Leyland Panthers.

The Corporation built four new bus depots in the 1960s as the tramway system contracted and the bus fleet expanded. Two, Maryhill (1962) and Partick (1964), were on the sites of former tram depots while the other two Gartcraig (1961) and Bridgeton (1965) were new operational sites. The former Bridgeton depot now houses the collection of the Glasgow Vintage Vehicle Trust. There were seven other bus depots around the city. The biggest was Knightswood with an allocation in the middle of the decade of around 220 buses.

Glasgow's buses were worked hard, and it was rare indeed for a GCT bus to find further use with another operator when its days in the city were over. Of its 515 early postwar purchases, all of which were withdrawn by 1967, only 15 would see service with other bus companies. These included Albion Venturers bought by Simpson of

Rosehearty, McKnight of Lanark and Dunoon Motor Services, and the Corporation's solitary Crossley DD42 which had been sold to AA of Ayr in 1957 when it was just ten years old.

A distinctive feature of the buses delivered to Glasgow from 1948 was the use of registrations in the FYS series, starting at FYS 101. This reached FYS 999 in 1959, when a new series started at SGD 1. This ended at SGD 739 in 1963, with new buses from 1964 having year-suffix registrations.

Glasgow Corporation had a protected operating area, roughly delineated by the city boundary, within which vehicles operated by the Scottish Bus Group could not carry local passengers. So, on inbound journeys, SBG services stopped only to set down passengers, and on journeys out of the city stopped only to pick up people making trips to points beyond the boundary.

Five of SBG's subsidiaries had depots around the city – roughly between six and ten miles out. Starting on the north bank of the

▲ From 1962 the standard Glasgow bus was the Alexander-bodied Atlantean, the first examples of which entered service in September that year, as the last of the city's trams were withdrawn. It's difficult to imagine the impact these stylish buses had in a fleet still running exposed-radiator AECs, Albions and Daimlers. LA184 (AGA 123B) is a 1964 bus, but is representative of almost 500 buses of this type delivered between 1962 and 1969. Most of Glasgow's 1960s Atlanteans carried Albion badges.

Clyde and going clockwise, these were located at Old Kilpatrick (Central SMT), Milngavie (Alexander), Kirkintilloch (Lawson), Stepps (Alexander), Baillieston (Scottish Omnibuses, opened in 1960), East Kilbride (Central), and Newton Mearns, Paisley and Inchinnan (Western SMT). At the start of the 1960s these nine depots operated around 750 vehicles, most of them buses, and many of them on services running into Glasgow. It's a very rough comparison, but add the vehicles operated by SBG's Glasgow area depots to the Glasgow Corporation bus and tram fleet and you get a total of around 2,400. Today, the nearest comparison is First's operations in Greater Glasgow plus the fleets of McGill's of Greenock and Stagecoach in Glasgow. Between them these three operators run around 1,100 vehicles.

There were five bus stations in the city, three used by SBG and one each by MacBrayne and Glasgow Corporation. The MacBrayne bus station was in Townhead, to the north-east of the city centre and a brisk 15-minute walk from the central area. The site is now covered by junction 15 of the M8 motorway. MacBrayne ran services from Glasgow to Fort William and on to Inverness, and down the Kintyre peninsula to Ardrishaig and Campbeltown. These were operated by coaches, with 1940s Maudslay Marathon IIIs being replaced by AEC Reliances as the decade progressed. MacBrayne was at this time Scotland's biggest Maudslay operator – it bought 34 between 1947 and 1949, all but one of which were still in service in 1960, including four which had been fitted with new Duple coach bodies in 1958-59. The first AEC Reliance had been delivered in 1958, and this model was one of the company's standard types

through the 1960s; there would be 38 in the fleet by 1969. There were also AEC service buses in the MacBrayne fleet, but these were not routinely seen in Glasgow.

The Glasgow Corporation bus station was in St Enoch Square, outside one of the city's four railway termini and close to the busy Argyle Street shopping area. It was used by services running south via the infamous Gorbals district to Toryglen, Kings Park, Castlemilk and Carmunnock.

None of the three SBG bus stations were what could really be called centrally located, because in the early 1930s the Corporation objected to private operators' buses penetrating the central area. There were two on the northern edge of the city – Buchanan Street, a

▲ Glasgow Corporation operated the Underground, which had been opened in 1896 by the Glasgow District Subway Company. The 4ft-gauge circular line was originally cable-hauled. It was taken over by the Corporation in 1922 and electrified in 1933. In the 1960s it was still being operated by the original Victorian rolling stock which had been built by the Oldbury Carriage & Wagon Co of Birmingham and Hurst Nelson of Motherwell. There were 15 stations on the 6½-mile route. This is Kinning Park.

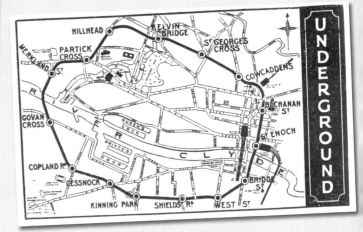

▲ Glasgow's 1959 livery with its yellow lower panels was prone to show dirt and minor accident damage, and in September and October 1964 a reversed livery was applied to 22 buses. This seemed like an improvement, but it was quickly abandoned and by early 1965 all of the buses had been repainted in the standard style. LA188 (AGA 127B) was the only Atlantean to be repainted, and the application of the revised livery to a bus just a few months old was presumably intended to see how it looked on a modern vehicle. Finding one of these 22 buses in a fleet of around 1,400 was a challenge for bus photographers.

▲ Glasgow's new standard bus featured on the cover of an improved version of the Corporation's timetable from 1963.

▲ A few prewar buses could still be seen in Glasgow at the start of 1960s. This Leyland Tiger TS8 in the Midland fleet was new in 1940, so strictly speaking was not prewar, but it was representative of many elderly Tigers, and survived until 1964, the year of this photograph. By having a short cab with an upright steering column, Alexander managed to squeeze an extra row of seats into its final TS8 Tigers, making them 39-seaters, rather than 35 as on previous deliveries. P682 (WG 9518) is parked outside Buchanan Street bus station on vacant land made available by the demolition of tenement blocks in 1963, and which provided valuable extra space for SBG in the city.

▲ Rare beasts indeed were Midland's two Willowbrook-bodied Leyland Tiger TS11s, new in 1942. Both were based at the company's Kilsyth depot and one was regularly seen in Glasgow's Dundas Street bus station on the Saturday afternoon 1D service which operated from Twechar via Muirhead, using one bus to provide a two-hour frequency. They were withdrawn in 1964. This is P684 (WG 9754).

covered terminal, and the nearby Dundas Street. Buchanan Street was confusingly referred to as Killermont Street by Central SMT. Dundas Street was on land now occupied by the Buchanan Galleries shopping centre, while the Buchanan Street terminal was slightly to the west of the present Buchanan Bus Station which opened in 1977 to replace the two northern bus stations.

Dundas Street was used almost exclusively by Alexander and by Lawson, which served the Kirkintilloch area using in the main Guy Arab III single-deckers and Bristol Lodekkas. The Alexander services operating from Dundas Street were primarily run by lowbridge Leyland Titans serving the Garthamlock housing estate on the eastern edge of the city, and by assorted other types operating longer distance services to Kilsyth, Falkirk, Dunfermline and Leven. Aside from the Alexander and Lawson services, Dundas Street provided a less than salubrious starting point for Western SMT's London service, and for holiday coach tours – described as Land Cruises – operated by Lawson.

Dundas Street was a utilitarian place, opened in 1944 and never significantly improved. The 1934 Buchanan Street bus station, with a glazed roof protecting buses and passengers, was better. The loading platforms were laid out in a fan shape, with buses being funnelled out through an entrance which only let one bus escape at a time, a recipe for peak-hour congestion and delays even before the departing buses got caught up in the traffic passing outside.

Buchanan Street was used by Alexander, with suburban services to the north-west edge of the city – Milngavie, Drumchapel – and to rural points beyond including Balfron and Aberfoyle and even Stirling by a circuitous route through Killearn and Balfron. Most of Alexander's services heading north-east out of Glasgow by the A80 road also left from Buchanan Street, running to Bo'ness, Stirling, Callander, Crieff, Dundee and St Andrews. In 1960 these

The vehicles which Midland acquired from David Lawson of Kirkintilloch were quickly repainted blue. Typical of Lawson's older buses is this 1947 Guy Arab III with Gardner 5LW five-cylinder engine and Duple 35-seat body. G9 (AMS 539) was one of 20 similar buses based at Kirkintilloch depot and carries the W Alexander & Sons (Midland) Ltd fleetname which was used for a short time in 1961–62 before the adoption of the script name seen on the Tiger in the previous photograph.

▼ Half-cab coaches became outdated almost overnight with the arrival at the start of the 1950s of new mid-engined models. Alexander addressed the issue by fitting ECW-style full-width fronts to two of its Burlingham-bodied CVD6s, and revising the side mouldings. Did it give the coach a more modern look in the eyes of the company's customers? It's hard to say, although most enthusiasts would probably be of the opinion that the half-cab coach on the left was more elegant than the full-front rebuild on MD34 (BWG 573). That only two Daimlers were treated this way suggests that Alexander decided the end result was not worth the expense.

▲ Still with Bluebird name and logo, this 16-year-old Burlingham-bodied Daimler CVD6 was a fine coach in its day, but that day was long past by 1965. In fairness, coaches of this type were seldom found doing anything other than peak-hour bus operation by this time, and D25 (BMS 420) is operating a short working to Glenboig on the Glasgow to Annathill service. All of Midland's Daimler coaches were withdrawn in 1965.

services were normally operated by Leyland Tiger Cubs and AEC Reliances which were usually, but not invariably, coaches.

From 1961 following the split of Alexander into three separate businesses, the Glasgow area operations, including those of Lawson, were taken over by Midland, with some of the long-distance services being jointly operated with Fife and Northern.

Many of Central SMT's Lanarkshire services operated from Buchanan Street, as did most of the Glasgow services of Scottish

▼ Alexander's last half-cab coaches were 20 Leyland Tiger OPS2/1s which were registered at the end of 1951 and entered service in 1952, just months ahead of the first of the company's Royal Tigers. The chassis were a cancelled export order and had been built in 1948, so were four years old before they turned a wheel. The OPS2 differed from the more common PS1 in having a bigger engine, the 9.8-litre O.600 in place of the 7.4-litre E181, and in being 8ft wide instead of 7ft 6in. The OPS2s were to be found in all three post-1961 Alexander fleets. These two coaches are working on summer Saturday express services. The Fife vehicle on the left has come from St Andrews in three hours, which is 49 minutes faster than the stopping service. The Northern coach on the right has come from Dundee, also in three hours, a 58-minute saving over the normal service. FBP7 (DMS 820) retains its original drive train; NPB2 (DMS 815) has been fitted with the engine, gearbox and axles from a PS1 and was one of 17 OPS2s so treated, releasing their original running units for use in the construction of new PD3 double-deckers as illustrated on page 61.

▲ A more modern style of vehicle on the St Andrews to Glasgow Saturday express was this Leyland-bodied Royal Tiger from the Fife fleet. FPC34 (DWG 691) was was one of ten purchased by Alexander in the spring of 1952 when the original buyer cancelled its order. In 1961 they were divided equally between Fife and Northern. The red and cream rubber mounting for the front windows is not original, nor is the lower front panel, indicative of recent accident repair work.

▲ Midland Lodekka MRD52 (KWG 605) leaves Glasgow on service 175 for Campsie Glen, a route operated by Lawson until 1961. It was an LD6G with 60-seat ECW bodywork. The fleetname was a trial version of the style which was used – but with bigger lettering – from 1965 to 1968.

▼ This is Cunningham Street, the terminus for the Scottish Omnibuses service to Easterhouse, one of the vast postwar municipal housing schemes built on the edge of the city. Alexander's Dundas Street bus station is behind the brick wall. In 1957 SOL purchased 20 Leyland Titan PD2/20s with attractive lowbridge Park Royal bodies and these spent their entire lives in the Glasgow area. They were the company's first new Leyland double-deckers since a solitary TD5 in 1942, and would be its last until Olympians in 1982. The conductor on HH554C (OWS 554) catches up with the day's news while sitting on the rear lower deck seat. The C suffix indicated a bus based at Baillieston depot, which opened in 1960.

▶ Three generations of Midland Titans with lowbridge Alexander bodywork lay over outside Buchanan Street bus station in 1965. In the foreground is a 1959 PD3, MRB197 (KWG 658). There were 92 lowbridge PD3s in the Midland fleet in the mid-1960s, of which 74 were based in three Glasgow area depots, Milngavie, Kilsyth and Stepps. On the left is a 1951 PD2, MRB135 (DMS 495), and in the right background is 1948 PD1 MRA46 (BWG 91). The PD3 was a 67-seater; the older Titans seated 53.

Omnibuses. The latter's hourly Edinburgh Express left from a stance in Germiston Street, outside the bus station.

Waterloo Street, opened in 1935, was another covered bus station, a couple of blocks west of Central Station and thus again on the periphery of the central area rather than in the heart of it. From here Central's services to Dunbartonshire were operated, along with some to Lanarkshire. A few Western SMT services also used Waterloo Street, principally to Mearnskirk, Ardrossan, Ayr via Kilmarnock, Carlisle and Stranraer.

In addition, each of SBG's subsidiaries had services which operated from on-street termini in the city. Close to Buchanan Street, Alexander services to Drumchapel departed from stops in Renfrew Street. Next to Dundas Street, Scottish Omnibuses' service to Easterhouse used Cunningham Street as a terminus. On the southern edge of the city centre there were terminal points on both banks of the River Clyde. Western services to Eaglesham, Neilston, Paisley and to destinations further afield including Gourock, Largs, Seamill and Ayr via Troon departed from Clyde Street on the river's north bank. These were all operated by double-deckers, mainly Leyland Titans and Bristol Lodekkas.

Western also had services running from St Enoch Square to Renfrew and points beyond, including Largs via Greenock. These started in the approach road to St Enoch Station.

Carlton Place, on the south side of the river, was the less than convenient starting point for some of Central's Lanarkshire routes, and for the Scottish Omnibuses service to Edinburgh via Salsburgh, one of three stopping services between Scotland's two biggest cities.

▼ Western SMT was the biggest user of the lowbridge Leyland PD3, with 186 in service from 1961 when its last 50 were delivered. These were PD3A/3s with the new St Helens glass fibre bonnet which echoed the style of grille used on the Vista Vue cab fitted to contemporary Leyland trucks. Inchinnan depot's ID1665 (RCS 363) has an Alexander body with platform doors, and is at the St Enoch Square terminus, where – shock, horror! – passengers boarded from the roadway rather than the pavement. The lower section of the grille has been replaced with mesh, probably because an overweight driver or conductor broke the original while using it as a step to reach the winding gear for the destination screen.

▼ Buses of acquired operators added interest to SBG fleets. This 1954 Leyland Titan PD2/12 – one of the last new Leyland-bodied buses in Scotland – was operated by Scottish Omnibuses and had been acquired in 1958 with the business of Lowland Motorways of Glasgow. The angle of the body suggests HH6C (LYS 757) was being driven with some verve, as it turns from Dundas Street into Cunningham Street on its arrival from Easterhouse. This busy service was the recipient of some of SOL's first 70-seat FLF Lodekkas in 1962.

▶ Central's acquisition of Chieftain of Hamilton was among the biggest of SBG's 1960s takeovers. Chieftain operated 31 buses, most of them Leyland double-deckers. HL209 (UVA 638) was a 1959 PD3/2 with forward-entrance 72-seat Massey body, an unusual layout for a small operator at this time. When it was delivered the only other forward-entrance double-deckers in Scotland were six Titans operating for Edinburgh Corporation. All of Central's double-deckers were lowbridge or lowheight, while most of Chieftain's were highbridge – so where appropriate they were given an H prefix to their fleet numbers to alert drivers to the extra height. Massey did a lot of business with Scottish independents in the late 1950s and early 1960s.

The slowest, via Wishaw, Shotts and Whitburn, took 2 hours 37 minutes giving an average speed of around 10mph – not that anyone would ever travel end-to-end on what was essentially a series of linked local services when the express took just 1 hour 25 minutes. By comparison the fastest train service from Glasgow Queen Street to Edinburgh Waverley, operated by green-liveried diesel multiple units, took just under one hour. In the mid 1960s the return fares were 18 shillings by train or 11s 6d by coach. The Edinburgh Express had one suburban stop in both Glasgow and Edinburgh, and then ran non-stop between the two cities via the A8 which for much of the 1960s had significant three-lane stretches, with the centre lane being used for overtaking by vehicles travelling in either direction, a high-risk layout even at a time when the roads were less busy than they are now.

The big change to SBG services running from Glasgow in the 1960s was the arrival of the Alexander Y-type. Early Y-types were used mainly as coaches, but from 1964 36ft-long Y-type Leopards (and, to a lesser extent Reliances) supplanted older types of vehicles on many inter-urban routes. Forward-entrance Lodekkas and Lowlanders appeared on services operated by Central, Midland and Western from 1962, followed by Fleetlines with stylish Alexander bodies running for Midland and Western from the middle of the decade. ■

▲ Carlton Place was the starting point for some of Central's services to Newton and Cambuslang, and is the location for this view of one of the company's two ex-Chieftain Atlanteans, with the River Clyde in the background. Although buses with this style of Metro-Cammell body were common in England, the two operated by Chieftain were the only Metro-Cammell-bodied Atlanteans bought new by a Scottish company. New in 1960, HR1 (XVA 444) was operated by Central until 1969. Chieftain owned two Atlanteans when it was acquired by Central in 1961, giving first Chieftain and then Central the unlikely distinction of, briefly, running Scotland's biggest Atlantean fleet.

◀ Vehicles which had been transferred between SBG companies were interesting too, especially elderly vehicles like the 14 PD1s which Scottish Omnibuses acquired from Central in the winter of 1961–62 when they were 15 years old. There had been no PD1s in the SOL fleet, which made them even more unusual. Northern Counties-bodied HH11B (BVD926) was based at Bathgate but is operating from Baillieston depot on the 215 to Airdrie and Clarkston, its destination being shown by paper bills on the nearside front window.

◄ ▲ Scottish Omnibuses' first 30ft-long double-deckers were 25 FLF6G Lodekkas with 70-seat ECW bodies, delivered in 1962. They were also the company's first forward-entrance double-deckers. Buses allocated to Baillieston depot were normally used on local services in Glasgow but on occasion found themselves being sent further afield. This 1965 view of AA871C (YWS 871) shows it after arriving in Glasgow on the Edinburgh Express, freshly repainted in Lothian green. The service was normally operated by AEC Reliance coaches but at peak times rather less luxurious vehicles would be used to provide extra capacity. Many SOL Lodekkas had Cave-Browne-Cave heating, identifiable by the air intakes on either side of the destination display. An even more unusual vehicle to find on the Edinburgh Express was Baxter's HH44V (XVA 276), one of four Leyland Titans which were the only new forward-entrance lowbridge buses for a Scottish operator. Delivered in 1960 and 1961, they had 56-seat Massey bodies.

▼ Western SMT's front-line coaches were painted black and white, and always looked smart. A 1955 Alexander-bodied Guy Arab LUF, based in Dumfries, is seen in Glasgow on a private hire. DG1108 (GCS 182) was a 41-seater. The glass louvres above the side windows were a nice touch, designed to reduce draughts when the sliding windows were open. Western's LUFs had Gardner 6HLW engines. A note on the decency screen beside the entrance warns: "Passengers entering or leaving this bus while it is in motion do so at their own risk."

▶ Waterloo Street bus station was a short distance from Central Station. The building in the right background is the Central Station Hotel. In 1964 Central SMT, whose fleet was predominantly double-deck, took 19 Leyland Leopards with 53-seat Y-type bus bodies, including T23 (AGM 623B). They marked quite a transformation for Central's passengers as they replaced lowbridge 53-seat double-deckers on routes such as that between Glasgow and Balloch. Single-deckers in the Central fleet seemed an oddity in 1964, but SBG's dissatisfaction with rear-engined double-deckers saw the company buying increasing numbers of 53-seat Leopards from 1967, and by the end of the 1960s it would be running 89. That number would grow rapidly in the 1970s.

▼ Scottish Omnibuses and Western SMT between them took 66 Bristol RELH6Gs in 1966, all with Alexander Y-type bodies which had a revised grille to provide an adequate airflow to the front-mounted radiator. Most of them were used on services to England, primarily from Edinburgh and Glasgow to London. Here two are loading in Glasgow on the overnight service to Bournemouth, which ran once a week, southbound on Fridays, northbound on Saturdays. The 450-mile journey was scheduled to take 14 hours 55 minutes. XA163/5H (EWS 163/5D) were 38-seaters with toilets (indicated by the X prefix to the fleet number) and had back-lit fleetname panels on the side.

▼ Scottish Omnibuses bought two batches of Bedford VAMs in 1966–67, 20 Alexander-bodied VAM5s, followed by 20 Willowbrook-bodied VAM70s. They were intended for rural operation, but from time to time could be found on distinctly urban services. Edinburgh-based ZC258A (LFS 258F) is leaving Buchanan Street bus station for Airdrie, not quite the type of service it had been purchased for. The Z prefix had been introduced by SOL in 1965 to identify dual-purpose coaches.

SBG was the biggest Scottish user of PD3A Titans, with 75 being delivered in 1961, all with 67-seat lowbridge bodies. They were Scotland's last new lowbridge buses. They included 18 with Alexander bodies for Midland. MRB274 (SWG 630) is seen here outside the company's Glasgow hires and tours office at the corner of Cathedral Street and Dundas Street, offering high capacity but minimal comfort on a Mystery Tour. Waiting passengers can be seen queuing behind the bus, while an Austin Cambridge in fashionable two-tone paint scheme passes. The lettering on the office promotes Omnibus Services (an archaic description by the 1960s) and Coach Tours; the Titan is perhaps a compromise – Omnibus Tours. This section of Dundas Street survives today, although not easily recognisable.

St Helens-style Titans

In 1960 Leyland introduced a revised new-look bonnet for its Titan range, which was made of moulded glass fibre rather than pressed metal, and had a sculpted nearside corner to improve the driver's view of the kerb. Generally known as the St Helens front, after one of the first users, a total of 83 Titans of this style were supplied new to five Scottish operators.

A1 Service	7
Alexander Midland	18
Alexander Northern	7
Glasgow Corporation	1
Western SMT	50

All were 30ft-long PD3As except for the seven A1 buses, which were 27ft-long PD2As. The sole Glasgow bus, L398, was an exhibit at the 1960 Commercial Motor Show at Earls Court, London. ∎

The Lowlander

There was by the late 1950s a general acceptance that lowbridge buses were not ideally laid out. A passenger sitting on the nearside of the upper deck on a busy bus had to squeeze past three others to reach the gangway. Those on the offside of the lower deck risked bumping their heads on the sunken gangway which intruded into the lower saloon.

To continue its policy of dual-sourcing double-deckers from Bristol and Leyland, the Scottish Bus Group convinced Leyland to build a lowheight model, which was launched at the 1961 Scottish Motor Show as the Lowlander. The first chassis, with forward-entrance Alexander body, was exhibited at the show in Western SMT livery.

The low-frame chassis was new, as was the drop-centre rear axle. There was a choice of gearboxes, Leyland's four-speed synchromesh or semi-automatic Pneumocyclic. Having specified manual gearboxes on all of its Titans, it was a surprise when SBG opted for the Pneumocyclic for most of its

72/74 seat double-deck bus chassis

Albion Lowlander

forward or rear entrance—single-level gangways lower & upper saloons

◄ The cover of Albion's Lowlander brochure featured a mock-up of the front part of an Alexander body.

Lowlanders. A few chassis were built with air suspension on the rear axle.

To minimise development costs Leyland retained the front end layout of the PD3A Titan, which meant a comparatively high-set driver's cab. The cab floor was 37 inches above the ground, compared with 33 inches for the floor in the Lodekka cab. Four inches might not sound much, but it forced compromises on the Alexander body, with the four front seats on the upper deck mounted six inches higher than the rest. With Alexander's standard front dome there was only room for a single-line destination and route number display on the first two Lowlander bodies – one for Western, the other a demonstrator in Glasgow Corporation livery.

▶ The first Lowlander had a 72-seat forward-entrance Alexander body, generally similar to bodies the company had built on Dennis Loline chassis for Aldershot & District, but with a single-line destination display. After being exhibited at the 1961 Scottish Motor Show it entered service with Western SMT in May 1962, as N1703 (TCS 151). It had a short life with Western, being transferred to Highland Omnibuses in 1966. It is seen in Clyde Street, Glasgow, one of the main terminal points for Western services in the city. The advert on the side promotes the company's Glasgow to London daily luxury coach service with a one-way fare of 50 shillings (£2.50).

◄ Central SMT's first Lowlander, A1 (EGM 1), was an exhibit at the 1962 Commercial Motor Show and its Northern Counties body had some detail differences from others in the batch such as cream rubber for the window mountings. Northern Counties coped rather better than Alexander with the Lowlander's high driving position, creating a neat-looking vehicle. Central had 20 Northern Counties-bodied Lowlanders, and 34 similar buses were supplied to Western. The illuminated advertising panel was a short-lived feature which was specified on a small number of buses in the early 1960s. It was back-lit by fluorescent tubes. Central's A1 loads in Glasgow's George Square in 1964 on one of the services linking the city with East Kilbride new town. It would be transferred to Alexander Fife in 1965.

▼ Two Alexander-bodied Lowlanders were delivered to Alexander Northern in April 1963. They were the company's first forward-entrance double-deckers, the first double-deckers to be delivered in yellow, and would be the company's last new double-deckers for 15 years. When new they were based in Aberdeen and were used mainly on the busy cross-city service 2 between Culter and Dyce, where they operated alongside lowbridge PD3s. The maroon wings were non-standard and would later be painted black. They were 71-seaters.

Production Alexander bodies were modified with raised front upper deck windows to make space for SBG's standard triangular destination display, but still had an untidy seating arrangement at the front of the upper saloon. Northern Counties produced an altogether neater body for the new Albion, and supplied examples to Central and Western. The first Central vehicle was exhibited at the 1962 Commercial Motor Show at Earls Court in London.

To coincide with the Lowlander's launch SBG announced orders for 106 for delivery in 1962, but very few arrived in that year, with volume deliveries only getting under way from early 1963. The Lowlanders had been slow to appear and were something of a disappointment when they did. Central, which operated 30, got rid of its whole fleet in 1965 with 18 going to Fife and 12 to Highland. Fife had 18 Bristol Lodekkas on order for 1965 and these were diverted to Central in place of the Lowlanders.

There was some disenchantment, too, at Western, which with 111 had the biggest fleet of the type. It withdrew 32 of its 1962–63 models in 1966–67 and, as with the unwanted Central buses, the recipients were once again Fife (which received 14) and Highland (18). Yet after this early flurry of activity, Lowlanders settled down to work full 16-year lives and the last Western examples survived until 1979.

Total Lowlander production amounted to just 274 vehicles, 193 of which went to SBG with 54 being bodied by Northern Counties and the remainder by Alexander. The chassis were assembled at Albion's factory in Scotstoun using kits of parts supplied by Leyland. ■

▶ Fife had seven new Alexander-bodied Lowlanders in 1963, but from 1965 expanded its Lowlander fleet with 32 buses transferred from both Central and Western. These entered service in their previous owners' liveries, as illustrated by ex-Western FRE34 (UCS 620) with Northern Counties body leaving Edinburgh for Dunfermline in 1967, operating via the Forth Road Bridge which had opened in 1964 and which led to new cross-river services being introduced by Fife and Scottish Omnibuses.

Edinburgh and the Lothians

Edinburgh Corporation ran Scotland's second-biggest municipal bus fleet, which stood at just over 700 vehicles in the mid-1960s serving a population of 467,000. (Today's Lothian Buses runs around the same number, but the city's population – in contrast to Glasgow's – has grown, and is now 495,000.) The fleet was fairly standardised, with 300 virtually identical Leyland Titans with Metro-Cammell Orion bodies accounting for just over half of the operator's double-deckers, and making Edinburgh one of the biggest buyers of the Orion. Where Glasgow had embraced Leyland's Pneumocyclic semi-automatic gearbox when it started buying Titans in 1956, Edinburgh stuck

▲ The last big Scottish order for Guys was placed by Edinburgh, for 70 Arab IVs with Gardner 6LW engines and 63-seat Alexander bodies. These handsome buses were overshadowed by the more numerous Orion-bodied Leyland Titans delivered around the same time. As the fleet moved increasingly towards Leylands, the non-standard Guys were withdrawn prematurely after 13 years; Titans delivered at the same time ran for up to 20 years. 935 (NSF 935) unloads in York Place. The yellow board below the front nearside window promotes greyhound racing at Powderhall Stadium from 6.30pm. A rare Austin Metropolitan is among the cars parked on the opposite side of the street and another Austin, an A55 Cambridge, is in the foreground.

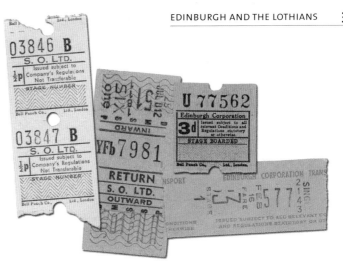

with manual gearboxes, only choosing the Pneumocyclic for a few trial buses and then for its final batch of 25 Titans in 1966. Glasgow selected the Atlantean as its standard bus in 1962; Edinburgh did not do so until 1966 – but did so with added style, specifying panoramic windows on all its Atlanteans from 1967.

When Leyland replaced its original new-look bonnet with what became known as the St Helens front in 1960, Edinburgh continued to have its Titans fitted with the older style grille. It also, at the start of the 1960s, modernised older exposed-radiator Titans with new-look fronts.

Edinburgh's oldest buses in 1960 were rebodied wartime Guys and Daimlers. There were also sixty 1953 rebuilds of ex-London

▼ At first glance this bus in St Andrew Square might look like a Leyland Titan PD2, but this strange concoction in the Edinburgh fleet is in fact a Daimler. 370 (DWS 547) started life in 1944 as an AEC-engined CWA6 with a Northern Counties body. In 1954 it was fitted with a Gardner 5LW engine and a new Alexander body with a pretend full-width front (there's no nearside glazing) and a new-look front which was updated in 1959 with this Leyland-style grille. It was one of 16 similar rebuilds. Edinburgh got its money's worth from the Daimler rebuilds which were not withdrawn until 1967.

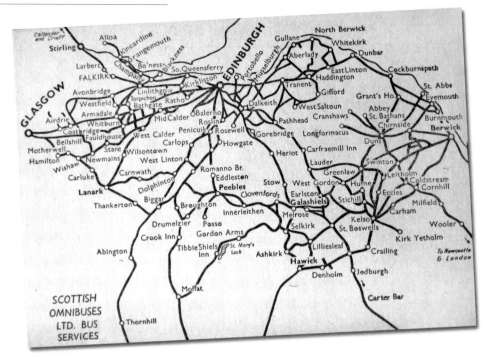

▼ Edinburgh bought 72 Daimlers in 1949–50, a mixture of CVG6s and CVD6s, all with Birmingham-style Metro-Cammell bodies. They served the city until the mid 1960s. The intermediate blind on 127 (FSC 174) reads "Part route" a peculiar feature of Edinburgh buses, presumably shown in the expectation that would-be passengers looked at the route number but didn't always check the final destination display. Where most operators carried fleet numbers on the front and rear of their buses, Edinburgh did not. They were instead located on the nearside, ahead of the entrance, and on the offside, to the rear of the cab door.

Transport Guy Arab IIs which had new Duple bodies and new Edinburgh registrations. All of these buses were modernised with Leyland-style new-look fronts in 1959.

Like Glasgow, Edinburgh had bought a variety of types in the late 1940s. Most were still in service in 1960 and included 72 Daimler CVG5s, CVG6s and CVD6s with Birmingham-style Metro-Cammell bodies, plus smaller numbers of AEC Regent IIIs, Guy Arab IIIs and all-Leyland PD2s. The Leylands were stock vehicles supplied by dealer Scottish Commercial. The predominance of Titans in ECT's mid-1950s buying overshadowed Guy's last big Scottish bus order, 70 Alexander-bodied Arab IVs delivered in 1956.

Edinburgh experimented with 30ft-long double-deckers and in 1960 there were six in the fleet, all forward-entrance Alexander-bodied PD3s, including one with a unique Homalloy bonnet and grille.

Single-deck buses played a relatively small part in Edinburgh's municipal transport. In 1960 there were a few rear-entrance Daimler CVG6s, Guy Arab IIIs and Bristol L6Bs, while in course of delivery there were 100 Leyland Tiger Cubs with Weymann bodies, ECT's biggest-ever intake of single-deckers. Delivery of these buses had started in March 1959 and would be spread through to January 1961. The first 50 were sold when just seven years old, being bought by Ulsterbus – apart from two accident victims which had been withdrawn earlier.

There were coaches too, although in 1960 these were an odd mixture. The coach fleet numbered 22 vehicles of which just three Alexander-bodied Tiger Cubs were purpose-built coaches. The rest were rebuilt buses and comprised 17 Leyland Royal Tigers, one Albion Aberdonian, and a Leyland Olympic which was the only

Between 1948 and 1950 SMT bought 80 new AEC Regent IIIs. The 20 Regents delivered in 1950 were bodied by Burlingham of Blackpool, a major supplier of single-deck bodies to SMT group companies in the late 1940s. These were the first buses to feature the triangular destination display which would become the group standard for double-deckers. It is similar to the style which was used by Ribble Motor Services and it is tempting to think that SMT's choice was influenced by bodies which Burlingham was building for Ribble at the same time as the Regents. The translucent roof panels were an unusual feature for a Scottish bus. BB96A (GSF 679) is seen in the dark green livery introduced in 1964.

◄ Curvaceous Duple bodies were fitted to 20 Regent IIIs delivered to SMT in 1949. BB74I (GSF 657) lays over in Bathgate. The metal mouldings above the lower deck windows were a Duple hallmark and an early example of a coachbuilder adding a touch of style to double-deck design. These buses were operated for 17 years. Scottish Omnibuses indicated double-deckers by using two prefix letters – B was an AEC single-deck, BB an AEC double-deck. The I suffix was the depot code for Broxburn.

▶ Unique is an oft misused word, but it does apply to this Leyland Tiger Cub in the Stark's fleet, photographed in York Place on its way to the bus station. It started life as a demonstrator and the 45-seat Alexander body was a one-off, quite different from the bus bodies the company would build on later Tiger Cub chassis. EWG 240 was new in 1953 and is seen after the Stark's business had been purchased by Scottish Omnibuses in 1964, carrying SOL fleet number H5S – the S indicating Stark's Dunbar depot. It was sold in 1967. The French-registered Renault Dauphine parked on the right has the yellow-tinted headlamps which were a requirement of the French authorities until the 1990s. Traprain – the sticker in the windscreen – is a hamlet a few miles from Dunbar.

▼ The Bristol Lodekka was the standard Scottish Omnibuses double-decker from 1956 to 1967 and could be seen in most parts of the company's territory. AA648A (RSC 648) is a 1958 LD6G, one of 152 delivered between 1956 and 1961, after which the company switched to FS and FLF variants of the Lodekka. It is in Edinburgh waiting to take up a trip to Queensferry Ash. The "Ash" in the destination was an abbreviation for Ashburnham Road.

example of the type supplied new to a Scottish operator. Where the buses were maroon (described as madder) and white, the coaches were white and black.

The coach fleet would undergo remarkable change at the start of the decade, with 22 smart new Duple-bodied Bedfords in 1963–64 replacing the odd collection of rebuilt buses. The Bedfords were a mixture of 25-seat VAS1s, 41-seat SB5s, and 52-seat VAL14s. More would follow towards the end of the decade by which time Edinburgh's coach fleet numbered 32 vehicles, mostly Bedfords but including two Ford R226s.

Edinburgh did not buy new buses every year, but when it did, it ordered them in neat batches of 50. Thus there were 50 PD2s in 1962, 50 PD3s in 1964, a split order in 1966 of 25 PD3s and 25 Atlanteans, 50 Atlanteans in 1967, and a further 50 in 1969. All of these had Alexander bodies. The last exposed-radiator buses – Daimler CVG6s – were withdrawn in 1967.

One thing which distinguished Edinburgh Corporation was the high standard of presentation of its vehicles, even the older members of the fleet. This was in sharp contrast to Glasgow, where the city's municipal buses often looked a bit worse for the wear. Edinburgh Corporation's buses were divided between five depots with that at Longstone in the south-west suburbs being one of Scotland's biggest, housing over 250 vehicles.

Edinburgh's out-of-town services were in the main operated by Scottish Omnibuses, running from the open-air bus station in St Andrew Square, complete with an exit featuring a colonnade to lend the humble bus station an air of grandeur in keeping with the general architectural ethos of the area. With hindsight it might seem a tad pretentious, but in mid-20th century Edinburgh it was just part

▼ Looking pretty much like a standard SBG vehicle, Alexander-bodied Leyland Tiger PS1 H3A (SS 7525) was an odd bus to find in the Scottish Omnibuses fleet in 1967. It was similar to Tigers delivered to Alexander in the late 1940s and 1950s, but stood out in the SOL fleet where AEC Regals dominated. The Tiger had been new to Stark's in 1950. It has just passed through the colonnade which fronted St Andrew Square bus station. When it was withdrawn in 1967 it was SOL's last half-cab single-decker; the last of the Regals had been taken out of service in 1966.

Alexander-bodied AEC Reliances of this style were purchased
by Alexander, Highland Omnibuses and Scottish Omnibuses. The
1961 Scottish Omnibuses vehicles were painted in bus livery as seen
on B833D (WSC 833); other years' deliveries were in predominantly
cream coach livery. The last Reliances of this style were purchased in
1962, after which the Y-type reigned supreme. This bus has arrived
on the two-hourly service from Hawick, which twice a day was
extended through to Carlisle, a journey of 4¼ hours.

of the street scene. In 1960 the Scottish Omnibuses livery was pale
green and the fleetname was SMT – for Scottish Motor Traction – set
on a distinctive diamond logo.

Most of the vehicles in the SMT fleet were AECs and Bristols. The
AECs ranged from front-engined Regals and Regents to underfloor-
engined Regal IVs, Monocoaches and Reliances. The Bristols were
Lodekkas, LSs and MWs. All of the company's Bristols had Gardner
engines. Alexander's buses ran in to Edinburgh from Callander,
Crieff and Stirling, and, in the summer, from Aberdeen.

Stark's Motor Services of Dunbar operated into Edinburgh, with
its buses carrying SMT fleetnames. Its livery was also green and
cream, but different shades from those used by Scottish Omnibuses.
And its newest buses, Reliances and Tiger Cubs with Alexander
bodies, were similar to those supplied to SBG. But despite the close

▶ Scottish Omnibuses
operated day excursions
and holiday coach tours
from Edinburgh. Its 1960
tours brochure shows a
Burlingham-bodied
Bedford OB on the
turntable ferry at Kyle of
Lochalsh. The Bedford was
one of 20 which had been
new in 1947–48 with SMT
Vista bodies and which
were rebuilt to forward
control and rebodied by
Burlingham in 1953.

▼ Edinburgh added 370 double-deckers to its fleet between 1954 and 1957, in part to replace the city's trams, after which double-deck purchases slowed down. Just six were delivered in 1958–59, before routine fleet renewal recommenced in 1962, with 50 Alexander-bodied Titans starting with 601 (YWS 601). By this time the standard concealed-radiator PD2A had the St Helens-style front, but Edinburgh fitted its own older-style Leyland bonnets to these and to two subsequent batches of Titans in 1964 and 1966. Note the illuminated advert panel.

Scottish Omnibuses suffered frequent vehicle shortages and in the winter of 1961–62 acquired 14 Leyland Titan PD1s from Central SMT. These 15-year-old buses were SOL's first PD1s (another four would come from Western SMT in 1965) and were operated until 1965–66. HH18 (BVD 933) in Bathgate, with SMT diamond fleetname, had Leyland bodywork. A 1957 Lodekka stands in the background. The bus stop sign just visible to the right of the Titan advises: "Bents, Blackburn, Seafield, This Side".

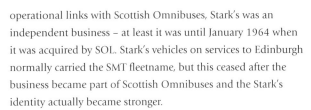

operational links with Scottish Omnibuses, Stark's was an independent business – at least it was until January 1964 when it was acquired by SOL. Stark's vehicles on services to Edinburgh normally carried the SMT fleetname, but this ceased after the business became part of Scottish Omnibuses and the Stark's identity actually became stronger.

The opening of the Forth Road Bridge in 1964 saw new services running between Edinburgh and key towns in Fife, most of which were operated jointly by Scottish Omnibuses and Alexander Fife.

Scottish Omnibuses went through an identity crisis in the early 1960s. It dropped the SMT diamond fleetname in 1963, replacing it with the word "Scottish". Then in 1964 it adopted a new and, it has to be said, rather drab, dark green livery – a shade called Lothian green which was harder-wearing than the previous light green. At the

◄ While Scottish Omnibuses was the dominant SBG operator in Edinburgh, vehicles of other SBG companies did serve the city. Northern Tiger Cub NPD11 (FMS 728) has arrived as a duplicate on the service from Aberdeen. This was routed via Stirling until the opening of the Forth Road Bridge, when it switched to using the bridge. This Tiger Cub was new in 1954 and was one of ten in the Northern fleet.

◀ Edinburgh's first Leyland Atlantean, 801 (ESF 801C), broke new ground by having panoramic windows on its Alexander body, an idea developed by recently-appointed general manager Ronnie Cox. It was exhibited at the 1965 Scottish Motor Show where it turned heads. All but one of the following 24 Atlanteans of this initial order had conventional windows, but big windows would be standard on subsequent orders. Edinburgh did not initially embrace the Atlantean wholeheartedly, taking 25 Leyland Titan PD3s – Scotland's last – at the same time as this bus was delivered.

same time the SMT diamond made a brief re-appearance before the company settled on Eastern Scottish as its trading name.

As elsewhere in Scotland, as the 1960s progressed so the Alexander Y-type became a common sight in Edinburgh, although most of those operated by SOL were AEC Reliances and Bristol REs, rather than the Leyland Leopards favoured by other SBG companies. Unusual single-deckers were Bedford VAMs bodied by Alexander and Willowbrook. These were intended for Borders area routes, but were often to be seen in the capital. Large-scale operation of rear-engined buses by Scottish Omnibuses did not start until the end of 1968 with the delivery of the first of two batches of Bristol VRTs.

Following a batch of Bristol RE coaches with Y-type bodies in 1966, at the end of the decade SOL introduced some of Britain's first 12m coaches, eight Bristol REMH models with a new body, the Alexander M-type, and a new livery, black and yellow. They were for the Edinburgh to London service. Similar coaches were delivered to Western.

Scottish Omnibuses' operating area extended south to the Scottish border, and east through Bathgate and Airdrie to Glasgow. Its depot in New Street, Edinburgh, was Scotland's biggest with a mid-1960s allocation of 275 buses and coaches. Apart from Stark's there were few independent operators running regular bus services in the Lothians or in the Borders area.

The Post Office introduced its first bus service in Scotland in June 1968, with a BMC J2 minibus running a circular service between Dunbar, Spott and Innerwick twice a day. Post Bus services would expand across much of Scotland in the 1970s. ∎

▼ In February 1965 Scottish Omnibuses tried a Bristol SUL4A demonstrator. This light-duty chassis had an Albion four-cylinder engine, as used in the Nimbus, and a spectacularly unattractive ECW 36-seat body with tiny windscreens. It was owned by the West Yorkshire Road Car Co, whose fleet classification SMA was curiously appropriate in Scots dialect where sma' is a corruption of small. SMA16 (EWT 385C) is seen leaving St Andrew Square bus station for North Berwick. It was also tried by Midland. No orders followed.

◄ Wiles of Port Seton operated local services and in 1966 bought three ex-Halifax Albion Nimbuses. RJX 259 was new in 1963 and had attractive 31-seat bodywork by Weymann. It is operating on a tour for the Scottish Branch of the Omnibus Society, whose board is displayed in the windscreen. In the summer months the OS Scottish Branch ran tours visiting the premises of accommodating operators, usually on Sundays. And most operators were accommodating at a time when the only nod towards health and safety legislation would be a warning not to fall in to the pits in the workshop.

▼ Between 1963 and 1969 Edinburgh added 32 new Duple-bodied coaches to its fleet. Most were Bedfords, but in 1968 as well as buying three Bedford VALs Edinburgh took a pair of Ford R226s. They were 52-seaters with Viceroy 36 bodies and were operated for seven years. 226 (MSF 226F) loads outside the Howard Hotel in Great King Street. The black and white livery for coaches had been introduced in 1955.

▲ Among the first Bristol VRTs to enter service anywhere in the UK were 25 which joined the Scottish Omnibuses fleet at the end of 1968. They were 33ft-long VRT/LL6G models and their ECW bodies seated 83, six more than on the standard-length buses which followed in the summer of 1969. These were the only long-wheelbase VRTs to be bodied by ECW. AA292A (LFS 292F) approaches Princes Street from Waverley Bridge. SBG's dissatisfaction with the VRT saw most going south to the National Bus Company in exchange for Bristol Lodekkas in 1973.

London link

When London Transport in the mid 1950s started to withdraw relatively young RT-class AEC Regent IIIs many headed to Scotland. Members of the A1 co-operative in Ayrshire bought large numbers, while the biggest user of the equivalent Leyland model, the RTL, was Chieftain of Hamilton. Dundee Corporation bought 30 of the non-standard Cravens-bodied RTs in 1956 to speed replacement of the city's trams.

A few RTs and RTLs found their way into Scottish Bus Group fleets via acquired operators. Central SMT ran 15 RTLs acquired from Chieftain; Scottish Omnibuses had six Craven RTs from Lowland Motorways, and Alexander Northern operated (but did not repaint) one ex-Simpson's RT.

Scottish operators who ran former London RTs or RTLs on regular service in the 1960s were:

	RT	RTL
A1	●	●
AA	●	●
Alexander Northern (ex Simpson's)	●	
Central SMT (ex Chieftain)		●
Chieftain		●
Clyde Coast	●	●
Cunningham's, Paisley	●	
Dundee Corporation	●	
Dunoon Motor Services		●
Garelochhead Coach Services	●	●
Irvine, Salsburgh	●	●
McConnachie, Campbeltown		●
McGill's, Barrhead	●	
McLennan, Spittalfield		●
Scottish Omnibuses (ex Lowland Motorways)	●	
Simpson's, Rosehearty	●	

Garelochhead Coach Services also operated three former London Transport RF-class AEC Regal IVs from 1964 to 1967–68, and A1 Service had a small number of 8ft-wide RTW-class Leyland Titans. ∎

▲ Dundee Corporation, which already operated AEC Regent IIIs, was quick to acquire 30 of London Transport's redundant Cravens-bodied RTs which were just seven years old when they were withdrawn from service. They were numbered 211 to 240, following on from a batch of new Daimlers, and entered service in Dundee in the summer of 1956 where they helped replace the city's last tram route, which ceased in October. Note that Dundee made use of the roof-mounted route number display. The RTs were withdrawn in 1968–69, when they were replaced by new Daimler Fleetlines. Dundee 225 (KGK 742) had been LT's RT1483.

▶ Over half – 73 out of 120 – of LT's Cravens-bodied RTs were bought by Scottish operators, including members of the A1 co-operative which had 25, as well as standard RT, RTL and RTW types. Hill & Paterson bought this six-year-old Cravens RT in 1956. A1 operators used variations of a blue, cream and maroon livery, and Hill & Paterson took some care with this bus with its striped radiator and its original rear wheel discs in place, in sharp contrast to the drab livery used by Dundee. The location is Irvine and KGK 772, previously London's RT1513, is on A1's trunk service from Ardrossan to Kilmarnock.

▶ This Clyde Coast RTL, JXC 20, was of note in that it entered service in 1948 as London Transport RTL501 and was in fact the first of the type to do so, in effect the prototype of the class. The numbers RTL1-500 were originally intended for 8ft-wide PD2s which were instead classified as RTWs. It was bought by A1 in 1958, passing to Clyde Coast in 1963. The location is Largs seafront; Largs was the northern terminus of Clyde Coast's 12-mile route from Saltcoats. There is still a bus stop and a pillar box at this location, although the Largs Hotel in the background has been converted to flats.

▼ Double-deckers were never commonplace on the Mull of Kintyre. McConnachie of Campbeltown operated just three, all in the 1960s, and two of these were ex-London Transport RTLs. LLU 907, with Metro-Cammell body, was new in 1950 as LT's RTL917. The McConnachie business was taken over by the town's other operator, West Coast Motor Services, at the end of 1969, and double-deck operation came to an end.

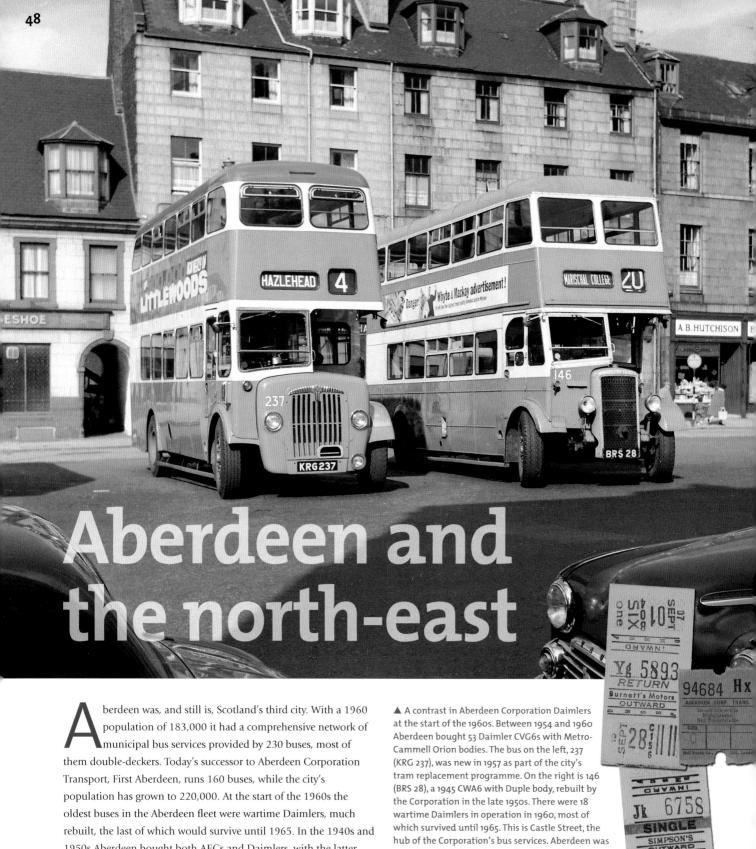

A contrast in Aberdeen Corporation Daimlers at the start of the 1960s. Between 1954 and 1960 Aberdeen bought 53 Daimler CVG6s with Metro-Cammell Orion bodies. The bus on the left, 237 (KRG 237), was new in 1957 as part of the city's tram replacement programme. On the right is 146 (BRS 28), a 1945 CWA6 with Duple body, rebuilt by the Corporation in the late 1950s. There were 18 wartime Daimlers in operation in 1960, most of which survived until 1965. This is Castle Street, the hub of the Corporation's bus services. Aberdeen was one of the first Scottish operators to match fleet and registration numbers, in 1934. It abandoned the policy for the duration of the war.

Aberdeen and the north-east

Aberdeen was, and still is, Scotland's third city. With a 1960 population of 183,000 it had a comprehensive network of municipal bus services provided by 230 buses, most of them double-deckers. Today's successor to Aberdeen Corporation Transport, First Aberdeen, runs 160 buses, while the city's population has grown to 220,000. At the start of the 1960s the oldest buses in the Aberdeen fleet were wartime Daimlers, much rebuilt, the last of which would survive until 1965. In the 1940s and 1950s Aberdeen bought both AECs and Daimlers, with the latter becoming the dominant supplier. The Regents included the only postwar RT-style models supplied new to a Scottish operator, along with conventional Regent IIIs. These were followed by Regent Vs, including five rare Gardner-engined examples.

There were just seven single-deck buses in the ACT fleet in 1960, Daimler CVD6s dating from 1947–48.

Aberdeen Corporation operated a range of city tours, generally using the newest double-deckers (some of which were fitted with public address systems) or two rebodied CVD6 coaches.

Daimler CVG6s were added to the fleet until 1965, after which Aberdeen switched to Daimler Fleetlines and Leyland Atlanteans. The operator's first-ever new Leylands were 12 Tiger Cubs in 1966–67, with unusual dual-door Alexander Y-type bodies. These

ABERDEEN CORPORATION TRANSPORT DEPARTMENT

TIME TABLE
FARE TABLE
STREET DIRECTORY
ROUTE MAP

▲ Aberdeen had 15 Weymann-bodied AEC Regent IIIs of this style, along with ten similar buses based on RT-type chassis as illustrated overleaf. A 1947 Regent, 27 (BRS 527), pauses at Byron Square while the conductor stamps his time card at the Bundy clock.

◀ Aberdeen's orders were split between AEC and Daimler in the 1940s and the 1950s. In 1950 and 1951 the Corporation took delivery of 35 Daimler CVG6s, including ten which were bodied by Brockhouse of Clydebank. Brockhouse supplied bodies of this style to all four of Scotland's municipal fleets. 35 (DRG 335) loads in Guild Street in 1964 on service 17 for Heatheryfold. A feature of most Aberdeen routes was a lunch-time peak. On route 17, for example, the daytime frequency was 10 minutes, but was halved to 5 minutes between midday and 2.30pm. All of the Brockhouse-bodied Daimlers were withdrawn in 1966.

▶ Between 1954 and 1957 Aberdeen bought 75 Daimler CVG6s with Birmingham-style new-look fronts. Of these, 35 were bodied by Crossley, including 177 (GRG 177) which was new in 1954. It is seen ten years later turning from Rosemount Viaduct into Union Terrace. The colourful Auto-Union 1000SP coupe in the background was powered by a three-cylinder 55bhp two-stroke engine.

◀ AEC supplied 30 Regent Vs to Aberdeen between 1955 and 1959 with bodies by Crossley, Park Royal, Metro-Cammell and Alexander. There were five of these attractive Park Royal-bodied buses, delivered in 1955, as illustrated by 251 (KRS 251). They were 66-seaters.

▼ The only new postwar RT-type AEC Regent IIIs in Scotland were ten delivered to Aberdeen Corporation in 1946–47 which were operated until 1965–66. They had Weymann bodies which were rebuilt towards the end of the 1950s, and upseated from 56 to 57 by replacing the first row of forward-facing seats in the lower saloon with a rearward-facing bench seat. 26 (BRS 526) pauses at the junction of Trinity Quay and Market Street.

were followed by AEC Swifts from 1968, the city's first AECs since Regent Vs in 1959. These were all one-man operated. More unusual one-man buses were a small number of Daimler CVG6 double-deckers which were rebuilt with forward entrances at the end of the decade. They were not an unqualified success. All of Aberdeen Corporation's buses were garaged in one large depot in King Street, the site today of the corporate headquarters of FirstGroup.

Aberdeen's buses were washed on a three-day cycle and each bus had a small coloured disc on the lower offside corner of the windscreen showing on which day it was to be washed.

Out-of-town services were provided by Alexander, and by three significant independent operators. The Alexander fleet was made up mainly of single-deckers, primarily AEC Regals and Reliances and Leyland Tigers, the oldest dating back to the mid-1930s. There were double-deckers – most of them Leyland Titans – operating on the

▶ Aberdeen Corporation switched from front-engined Daimler CVG6s in 1965 to rear-engined Fleetlines in 1966. These were the first rear-engined double-deckers anywhere north of Dundee, and like most Scottish Fleetlines had Alexander bodies. With the arrival of the Fleetlines Aberdeen started a new number series for double-deckers at 101. This is Guild Street in the summer of 1966 when the Fleetlines had just entered service. This brighter livery with the roof painted cream rather than grey had been introduced in 1965.

There were 20 PD3/3 Titans and seven PD3A/3s in the Northern fleet in the 1960s, all with 67-seat lowbridge Alexander bodies. The biggest concentration – 15 of the 27 – was in Aberdeen, and they were regular performers on the cross-city service between Culter and Dyce. The others were scattered around Northern's territory, from Dundee in the south to Elgin in the north. NRB228 (OMS 302) is a 1960 bus, and would be among the company's last Titans when it was withdrawn in 1977.

local cross-city service between Culter and Dyce, and on routes north to Buchan. There was no bus station in Aberdeen in 1960, and Alexander's services operated from a variety of bus stands around the city centre, most of them within easy walking distance of the main thoroughfare, Union Street, if not of each other. A new bus station opened in Guild Street in 1963, adjacent to the railway station.

The division of Alexander into three smaller units in 1961 saw services in the north-east of Scotland passing to the new Northern company, which in 1962 adopted a striking yellow livery. Within two years most of the fleet had been repainted. New vehicles were AEC Reliances, until 1964, after which the Albion Viking became the fleet standard. Only eight double-deckers were purchased by Northern in the 1960s – six PD3s in 1961 (delivered in Alexander blue), followed by two Albion Lowlanders in 1963.

Northern had five depots in Aberdeenshire, in Aberdeen, Fyvie, Huntly, Peterhead and Rosehearty, and three in the neighbouring counties of Kincardine (Stonehaven) and Banff (Buckie and

▲ Just arrived from Glasgow on the 6¼-hour limited-stop service via Forfar is one of Northern's impressive Alexander-bodied Leyland Royal Tigers, PC56 (EMS 511). It was new in 1953 and is seen in 1965, still on front-line duty. Coaches of this style could be found in all three Alexander fleets and similar vehicles, but on Guy Arab UF chassis, were bought by Central SMT and Western SMT and cascaded to Highland in the mid 1960s. The summer-only Glasgow to Aberdeen service was jointly operated by Northern and Midland.

▼ Northern advertised in Aberdeen Corporation's bus timetable, and in the 1968–69 edition used an illustration of a 1961 Tiger Cub, with a style of Alexander body unique to the Midland fleet. An Alexander Y-type, of which there were over 100 in service with Northern, would have seemed a more obvious choice.

▼ Alexander's bus body of the mid 1950s was a nicely-proportioned design and was built on AEC Reliances and Monocoaches for Alexander, Highland Omnibuses and Scottish Omnibuses, and on Leyland Tiger Cubs for Alexander. Northern's NAC92 (HMS 241), a 1956 Reliance, approaches Aberdeen bus station with its destination already set for the return journey to Methlick. Reliances of this type had 20-year operating lives with Northern.

Northern had two garages in Stonehaven, for an allocation of just 26 buses. The premises in Cameron Street, in the centre of the town, also served as a bus station, and that's where 1947 Regal NA49 (AWG 636) is seen on a summer evening in 1965. It was unusual in having a body built in Alexander's bus workshops in Brown Street, Falkirk, rather than at the coachbuilding factory in Drip Road, Stirling. Despite its immaculate appearance this bus was due for imminent withdrawal – although when it left the Northern fleet it headed south to spend 12 months with Scottish Omnibuses. The lady on the left is standing alongside a sign painted on the large green door behind her which advises "Queue here for Aberdeen direct".

◄ ▲ Outside the other Stonehaven depot, in Arbuthnott Place near the harbour, is smart 33-seat Burlingham-bodied Daimler D19 (BMS 414). Northern had four of these CVD6s. The two at Stonehaven were the only Northern half-cabs to be painted in coach livery while the other two, at Elgin, were in yellow bus livery, as illustrated by ND10 (BMS 405). New in 1948, all four remained in service until 1970.

▲ A local service in Stonehaven was provided by Invercarron Garage which from 1965 used this Bedford OLAZ with Duple body. KGD 909 had been new to MacBrayne in 1952 and was operated in its original owner's livery. Northern took over the service, but not the bus, in 1968.

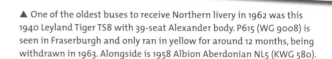

▲ One of the oldest buses to receive Northern livery in 1962 was this 1940 Leyland Tiger TS8 with 39-seat Alexander body. P615 (WG 9008) is seen in Fraserburgh and only ran in yellow for around 12 months, being withdrawn in 1963. Alongside is 1958 Albion Aberdonian NL5 (KWG 580).

▼ Simpson's Motors operated local services in the Fraserburgh area and through services to Aberdeen with a selection of generally elderly buses. A rare type to find in Scotland was this 1940 Bristol K5G, FLJ 543, with antiquated six-bay ECW lowbridge body. It had been new to Hants & Dorset, and was acquired third-hand by Simpson's in 1962 when it was already 22 years old and thus a prime candidate for the scrap-yard – so was presumably purchased at a bargain price. Simpson's ran it for two years.

Macduff). Further afield it also had depots in Moray (Elgin), Angus (Arbroath, Dundee, Forfar and Montrose) and Perthshire (Blairgowrie).

The biggest of the independents in the north-east was Simpson's Motors of Rosehearty, which operated from that town to Aberdeen, and also ran local services in Rosehearty and Fraserburgh, and 65 miles further west in Forres. Simpson's ran 30 buses, most of them old and second-hand. Its Aberdeen routes terminated in an open space in Mealmarket Street, which until the bus station opened in 1963 was also used by Alexander services heading north, and by another independent, Burnett's Motors of Mintlaw. Most of Burnett's vehicles were AECs, including two Regent IIIs bought new in 1950 which had the only double-deck bodies built by Federated Industries of Aberdeen. In 1960 Burnett was running a dozen buses.

The third of the big independents was Strachan's Deeside Omnibus Services, running to Ballater, the company's base, and Braemar. Between 1947 and 1950 Strachan's bought six new Foden single-deckers (its last new buses), and subsequently added used examples to its fleet. There were 11 Fodens in operation in 1960, plus one prewar Daimler.

All three of these companies were bought by Northern in the 1960s. The first to go was Strachan's, in May 1965. By this time the 12 vehicles in the fleet comprised seven Fodens, four AECs and one Leyland. The newest was an 11-year-old Reliance. All but two were quickly withdrawn by Northern. A statement made by the company's owner, Helen Strachan, when she announced the sale summed up the problem facing many operators running in rural areas: "We just cannot carry on—it is hopeless. I was in a bus yesterday and there were just half a dozen people on it, all short-distance passengers."

The Simpson's business was purchased by Northern in December 1966. Here there were 31 buses. Eleven were Bedford and Thames coaches bought new between 1960 and 1965. The remainder of Simpson's vehicles were second-hand AECs and Leylands from a variety of sources. Six of Simpson's vehicles served Northern long enough to be repainted yellow. Burnett's followed soon after, in January 1967. This was a smaller fleet, 14 AECs comprising four Regent IIIs, three Regal IIIs, and eight Reliances. Nine of these received Northern colours. ∎

▼ Alexander operated 14 Leyland Tiger PS1s with 33-seat Burlingham Sunsaloon bodies, and in the 1961 split of the company these were shared between Fife and Northern. These heavy-looking coaches entered service in 1950 and while the full-width front might have added a touch of modernity, the Tigers lacked the grace of the Burlingham-bodied Daimlers delivered two years earlier. There were nine in the Northern fleet and they were operated until 1971, retaining coach livery to the end. This is PA207 (CWG 334).

▲ Glasgow Corporation worked its buses hard and few found second lives with new owners. However Simpson's purchased seven Albion Venturers from Glasgow in 1962 – six for operation plus one for spares. They were 12 years old when they arrived in Rosehearty and served Simpson's for two or three years. EGA 98 has rare Scottish Aviation double-deck bodywork. A nice example of Simpson's economy is that only the lower deck has been repainted; the upper deck is in the lighter green the bus was wearing when withdrawn by Glasgow, complete with an advert for Crawford's Rich Tea Biscuits. A former London Transport RT stands in the background in Fraserburgh bus station.

In 1965 Simpson's adopted a brighter livery with cream window surrounds for its double-deckers, as seen on a 1947 RT-type AEC Regent operating the Fraserburgh town service in 1967 in Northern ownership. NRC1 (HLW 144) carries its Northern fleet number above the offside headlight. It was one of four former London Transport RTs purchased by Simpson's in 1963 from Leicestershire operator Brown's Blue. It ran for Northern until 1968, but was not repainted yellow.

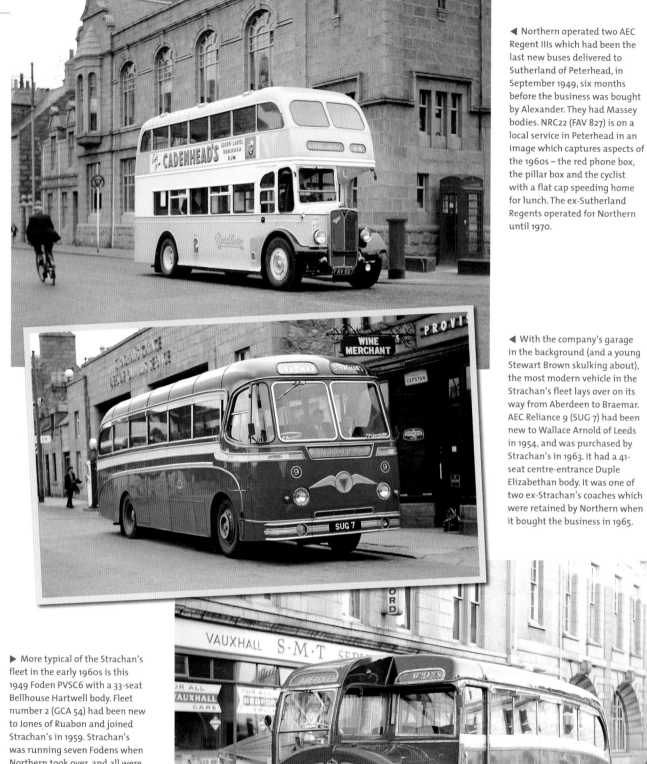

◀ Northern operated two AEC Regent IIIs which had been the last new buses delivered to Sutherland of Peterhead, in September 1949, six months before the business was bought by Alexander. They had Massey bodies. NRC22 (FAV 827) is on a local service in Peterhead in an image which captures aspects of the 1960s – the red phone box, the pillar box and the cyclist with a flat cap speeding home for lunch. The ex-Sutherland Regents operated for Northern until 1970.

◀ With the company's garage in the background (and a young Stewart Brown skulking about), the most modern vehicle in the Strachan's fleet lays over on its way from Aberdeen to Braemar. AEC Reliance 9 (SUG 7) had been new to Wallace Arnold of Leeds in 1954, and was purchased by Strachan's in 1963. It had a 41-seat centre-entrance Duple Elizabethan body. It was one of two ex-Strachan's coaches which were retained by Northern when it bought the business in 1965.

▶ More typical of the Strachan's fleet in the early 1960s is this 1949 Foden PVSC6 with a 33-seat Bellhouse Hartwell body. Fleet number 2 (GCA 54) had been new to Jones of Ruabon and joined Strachan's in 1959. Strachan's was running seven Fodens when Northern took over, and all were quickly withdrawn. This bus is seen at the Aberdeen terminus of Strachan's services, in Bon Accord Street. The Aberdeen branch of SMT Sales & Service, the Vauxhall and Bedford dealer, is in the background.

Sutherland bought both Leylands and AECs. The Leylands included six Tiger PS1s with 35-seat Duple bodies. NPA198 (EAV 459) is waiting at Gardenstown terminus on the service from Fraserburgh which Northern had taken over in 1966 with the Simpson's business. There was one trip each way on weekdays, and two on Saturdays.

▶ Between 1963 and 1965 Burnett's replaced half of its fleet with seven AECs purchased from City of Oxford Motor Services – three Regal IIIs and four Regent IIIs, all dating from 1950. They mainly replaced 1940s Albions, but also ousted the only double-deckers ever bought new by Burnett's, a pair of 1950 Regent IIIs with bodies by Federated Industries of Aberdeen. That second-hand 1950 Regents replaced the two owned since new suggests that the cost of re-certifying the Federated Industries-bodied buses was prohibitive. The Regal IIIs had 32-seat Willowbrook bodies and all were still in use when Northern took over in 1967. This is Northern NA107 (OJO 728). Two were withdrawn in 1968, but the third lasted until 1972, at which time it was one of the last half-cab single-deckers in SBG service.

Rebodying

Rebodying of old chassis was a common practice in the late 1940s and early 1950s as operators replaced wartime utility bodies with new and more comfortable bodywork built to higher quality standards. It usually, but not always, extended the lives of the vehicles so treated. The practice slowed down as the 1950s progressed, and had virtually halted by the start of the 1960s apart from the occasional rebodying of accident-damaged vehicles. ■

▶ Many of the buses rebodied in the early postwar years were utility Guy Arabs, such as this vehicle in the Alexander Midland fleet seen in Glasgow's Dundas Street bus station. The chassis dated from 1944; the 53-seat lowbridge ECW body from 1951. Prior to 1961 RO459 (AMS 46) had been part of the David Lawson fleet. Midland operated six of these rebodied Arabs, the last surviving until 1965.

◀ ECW bodywork was fitted to 15 Leyland Titan PD1s in the Western SMT fleet in 1952. When new they had carried Strachans bodies and the fact that they had to be rebodied after just three years in service speaks volumes about the quality of Strachans' construction. RD513 (CCS 411) is operating on Bute, and is seen in Rothesay, the island's main town, ready to depart for Ettrick Bay – a service which had been operated by trams until 1936. The former Rothesay Tramways Co depot at Port Bannatyne was used by Western as a bus garage, and still performs that function today for West Coast Motors. The bus carries an 'A' above the fleet number which in theory indicated 1950, although the chassis of this bus actually dated from 1949. This location, Guildford Square, is still a loading point for buses.

One of the more unusual rebodies for Scottish Omnibuses took place in 1954 when a 1949 Regent III, badly damaged in an accident, was despatched to the company's Marine Works and fitted with an angular new body which looked more like a product from 1944 than 1954. The extent of the rebuild saw the chassis being given a new number in the SMT series which had previously been used for Guy Arab rebuilds, and the bus, BB71, was also re-registered, becoming LWS 218. It was repainted in the new dark Lothian green livery in 1964 and was withdrawn in 1966. It carries the SMT diamond fleetname, unusual for a dark green bus. In its austere outline the Marine Works body is not dissimilar to the 1948 Alexander body on the Regent III visible in the background in Edinburgh's St Andrew Square bus station. It's tempting to imagine the bodyshop foreman at Marine Works pointing to an Alexander-bodied bus and telling his workers: "Build one just like that."

▼ In 1948–49 SMT took delivery of 55 AEC Regal IIIs with half-cab Alexander coach bodies. The advent of a new generation of underfloor-engined coaches rendered the Regal IIIs obsolete after just a few years in service, and to prolong their front-line lives 35 were fitted with new full-fronted Burlingham bodies in 1953-54, after having their chassis lengthened to 30 feet. By the 1960s they had been demoted to bus duties, as illustrated by B388D (GSF 707) leaving Edinburgh for Newtongrange, ten miles to the south. A new Ford Cortina is on the left in this 1965 view.

▶ AA member Dodds of Troon had an interesting approach to Guy Arabs which included a fair amount of rebuilding and body-swapping. This bus was one of three wartime Arabs which had been new to Plymouth Corporation and were purchased by Dodds in 1954. One was put into service, but the other two were stored and only entered operation with Dodds after being fitted with new bodies – this one, by Alexander, in 1957 and the other by Northern Counties in 1960. Both rebodied buses served Dodds for 13 years. Registrations KAG 573-575 were used for a trio of buses for AA members, each with similar Alexander bodies: a new Daimler CVG6 for Tumilty, illustrated on page 88, the rebodied Dodds Guy, and a new Leyland Titan PD2 for Young. Most Dodds buses carried DT (Dodds Troon) fleet numbers in the style shown on this bus in Ayr: D.T. No. 8.

In 1960 Aberdeen Corporation had ten 1951 Daimler CVG6s fitted with new 66-seat Alexander bodies, to replace their original 56-seat bodies by Northern Coachbuilders. The rebodied buses no doubt lasted longer than they would have had they retained their original bodies, but not any longer than other buses delivered around the same time. By way of comparison a batch of 15 Weymann-bodied Daimlers delivered in 1950 was withdrawn in 1969–70 after a mid-life rebuild in 1959–60 – an operating life of 19 or 20 years. Most of the 1951 Daimlers with their 1960 Alexander bodies were withdrawn in 1971, also a 20-year life. This is 165 (DRS 365) in Castle Street on the cross-city service 1, which ran from Balgownie to Garthdee.

▲ Neighbouring Ayrshire group A1 Service also had a few rebodied vehicles, including this Daimler CVD6, DCS 616, which started life in 1950 as an Irvine-bodied coach but after the expiry of its initial seven-year Certificate of Fitness was fitted with a smart new 61-seat Massey body in 1958. Massey bodies were supplied to a number of small Scottish operators around this time, including Baxter, Chieftain, Graham's and McGill's. A1 had a bus station in Kilmarnock, the location of this view. The Daimler's owner, Hunter of Dreghorn, took some trouble with the painting of the bus, with a thin maroon line separating the cream and the blue areas, and fine cream lining-out.

▼ In 1947–48 Aberdeen Corporation received seven Daimler CVD6 single-deckers which were bodied locally by Walker as rear-entrance 34-seaters. Five received major rebuilds during their lives, and the other two were fitted with new 35-seat Alexander bodies in 1958, the builder's last half-cab single-deckers. One of these was 11 (CRG 811), seen here at the sea front on a city tour. Aberdeen got its money's worth from the new bodies with the two vehicles running until 1971–72. As well as running city tours they were also used as one-man-operated buses.

◀ Between 1958 and 1961 MacBrayne had new Duple Vega-style coach bodies fitted to six old chassis – four ten-year-old Maudslay Marathon IIIs and two eight-year-old AEC Regal IIIs. The rebodied coaches were 7ft 6in wide, which made them more suitable for narrow Highland roads than new 8ft-wide vehicles. Two of the Maudslays had been operating with prewar Park Royal coach bodies which were some ten years older than the chassis, so were prime candidates for upgrading. Maudslay 140 (GUS 930) pauses in Glasgow's Parliamentary Road with the unprepossessing Lemon Tree pub in the background.

▼ Unusual deliveries to Alexander in 1960 were 17 Leyland Titan PD3s which were not quite what they seemed. Leyland supplied new chassis frames, into which Alexander fitted the running units – O.600 engines, gearboxes, axles – removed from a batch of Leyland Tiger OPS2 coaches which had entered service in 1952. The OPS2s were in turn fitted with the running gear from older PS1 Tigers, which were scrapped. The Titans were described by Alexander as PD3/3Cs, and were fitted with new 67-seat lowbridge Alexander bodies and allocated to Southern area garages, which meant all passed to Alexander Midland in 1961. Larbert-based MRB259 (RMS 691) loads in Falkirk's Callendar Riggs bus station for Fankerton carrying an experimental livery worn by just four buses in 1963–64. The Fankerton service was normally operated by one bus on a 70-minute frequency, upped to two buses every 35 minutes on Saturdays.

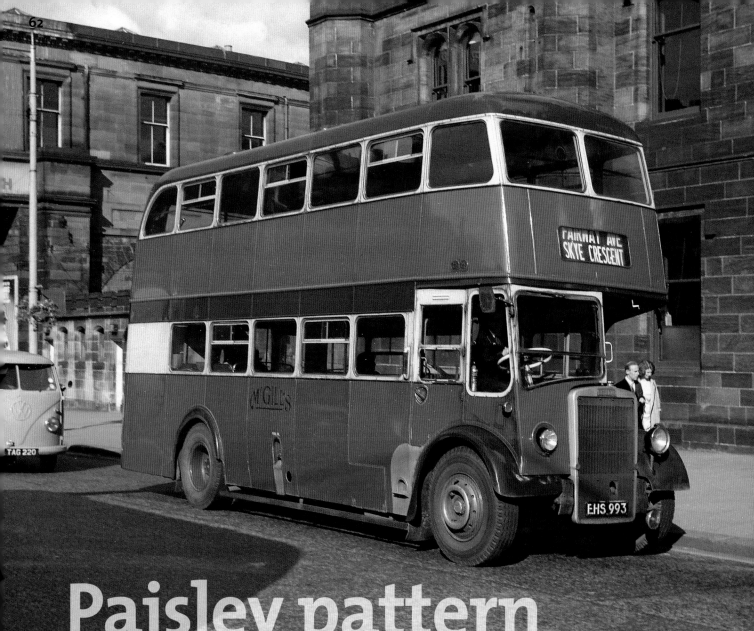

Paisley pattern

aisley was a colourful place in the 1960s. For most of the decade it was served by six bus operators. The biggest was Western SMT, which had become established as the main operator in the town with the purchase in 1951 of Young's Bus Service and the associated Paisley & District company. Between them they had operated 131 buses, many of which were still in the Western fleet in 1960 – Guy, Leyland and Daimler double-deckers.

The other five were independents. McGill's Bus Service of Barrhead was easily the smartest, with impeccable presentation of its fleet. Most of its 20 buses were bought new. Graham's Bus Service of Hawkhead was next, operating Guy Arabs in the main, bought

▲ In the late 1940s McGill's bought five Leyland-bodied Titans. The last of these was EHS 993, a PD2/1 which entered service in 1949 and is seen near the end of its life in Paisley in 1965. This version of the company's livery was phased out during the decade, as the company abandoned the maroon relief and the stylish fleetname.

both new and second-hand. Graham's ran 26 buses. The small fleet operated by Smith of Barrhead was also well turned out, and all of its vehicles were of lowbridge or lowheight layout because its route between Paisley and South Nitshill passed under a low railway bridge. Smith was owned by the Scottish Wholesale Co-operative Society, and also ran a coach fleet. The eight-vehicle Smith bus operation was taken over by Western SMT in 1968. The two other operators mostly bought second-hand buses. Cunningham's Bus Service ran ex-London RTs, which were succeeded by ex-Ribble PD2s, and then younger Titans from other sources. Cunningham's first new bus was an Alexander-bodied Leyland Atlantean in 1967. The fleet of Paton Bros of Renfrew was made up mainly of secondhand Leyland Titans from a wide range of operators. ∎

▲ In 1951 Western took delivery of 24 Daimler CVG6s, the chassis of which had been ordered by Young's of Paisley. They had lowbridge Alexander bodies and operated mainly from Kilmarnock and Johnstone depots. Johnstone-based JR940 (BSD 289) is on a Paisley local service.

▼ Paisley was one of the towns where Western SMT operated Guy double-deckers, a minority type in the fleet. These included Arab IVs with lowbridge Northern Counties bodies. JY1172 (GSD 693) was new in 1955 and had a Gardner 6LW engine.

▲ Graham's also operated Guy Arabs with Northern Counties bodies, but usually of highbridge layout. Nine new Arabs joined the fleet between 1949 and 1962. This Arab IV at Paisley Cross, 42 (XS 9834), was new in 1957 and is on the company's main route from Hawkhead to Linwood, the site from 1963 of the Hillman Imp car factory. The step on the front nearside wing helps the driver or conductor reach the winding handle for the destination screen.

▶ In the late 1950s McGill's patronised Massey Bros of Wigan, specifying its bodywork on one new Leyland Titan, the company's last, and on two Daimler CVG6s, all delivered in 1959. Massey had also rebodied four Guy Arab IIs for McGill's in 1955. By the mid-1960s these buses carried a simplified fleetname. This is McGill's depot in Muriel Street, Barrhead.

Typical of Cunningham's fleet in the early 1960s is 35 (HLX 224), an ex-London Transport RT-class AEC Regent III which was bought in 1958 when it was 11 years old, and was operated until 1968. It has a Saunders body. Cunningham's operated between Paisley and Renfrew Ferry, where this RT is seen. It was a high-frequency route run jointly with Paton and with less frequent participation by Western SMT and McGill's. The cars just visible in the foreground, a Ford Anglia on the left and the bonnet of an Austin with its distinctive flying-A badge on the right, are queuing for the chain ferry which until 1984 crossed the River Clyde to Yoker.

▼ After buying RTs Cunningham's switched to Leyland Titans. Ex-Ribble buses were popular in Scotland in the early 1960s. This was in part because Millburn Motors, the Glasgow-based dealer, had a branch in Preston and handled the onward sale of many redundant Ribble buses including this 1948 PD2/3 which in 1963 became Cunningham's 40 (CCK 624). Cunningham's had six of these CCK-registered Titans. Zoflora disinfectant remains on sale half a century after this photograph was taken.

▲ Most of Paton's buses in the 1960s were second-hand Leyland Titans, as illustrated by 86 (EN 9971), one of five ex-Bury Corporation PD2s with Weymann bodywork dating from 1950, which were purchased in 1964. This is the Paisley end of the Renfrew Ferry service and, like the Cunningham's RT illustrated opposite, the Paton bus has a destination screen which shows the names of both termini simultaneously, relieving the crew of the arduous task of changing the screen at the start of each trip. Although Paton only operated 30 buses, almost 70 second-hand Titans were purchased between 1960 and 1969, indicative of the high turnover and short lives of many of the company's elderly vehicles.

▶ Graham's bought second-hand Guys from a number of sources. In 1962–63 these included six Southampton Corporation buses, dating from 1948. They had 56-seat Park Royal bodies. Graham's made good use of the Southampton destination display, with the route number aperture showing 'via Paisley X', the location of this view. In the mid 1960s there were 21 Guy Arabs in the 26-vehicle fleet. A Ford Consul Classic is parked on the far side of the road.

▶ The Smith bus fleet numbered eight vehicles, all bought new. There were four lowbridge Leyland Titan PD2s, and four lowheight AECs, two Renowns and two Bridgemasters. The Bridgemasters, new in 1961, had 72-seat Park Royal bodies and were the first forward-entrance double-deckers in Paisley. 29 EGD stands at Smith's terminus behind Paisley Abbey in Cotton Street, a name acknowledging what was once one of the town's main industries.

▼ The last new Guy bus for a Scottish fleet entered service with Graham's in 1964. It had been an exhibit at the 1962 Commercial Motor Show, where it signalled the return of Strachans to the production of double-deckers, and was the only rear-entrance bus on show. However with 73 seats it failed its tilt-test and had to be down-seated to 69 by removing one row of seats from the top deck before it could be operated. It was the only new Arab in Scotland to have the short-lived Johannesburg-style grille. 56 (FXS 601) served Graham's until 1977 and then spent a couple of years with Crawford of Neilston. It was Graham's first 30ft-long double-decker.

▲ The first forward-entrance double-decker for Cunningham's arrived in 1964. 42 (LSN 286) was a Daimler CSG6/30 with a synchromesh gearbox and a 74-seat Northern Counties body. It had been an exhibit at the 1959 Scottish Motor Show, and was then bought by Garelochhead Coach Services, entering service in 1960. It was considerably younger than any other buses in the Cunningham's fleet which were all more than 12 years old. It had a short life with Cunningham's, being sold in 1967 and replaced by a new Leyland Atlantean.

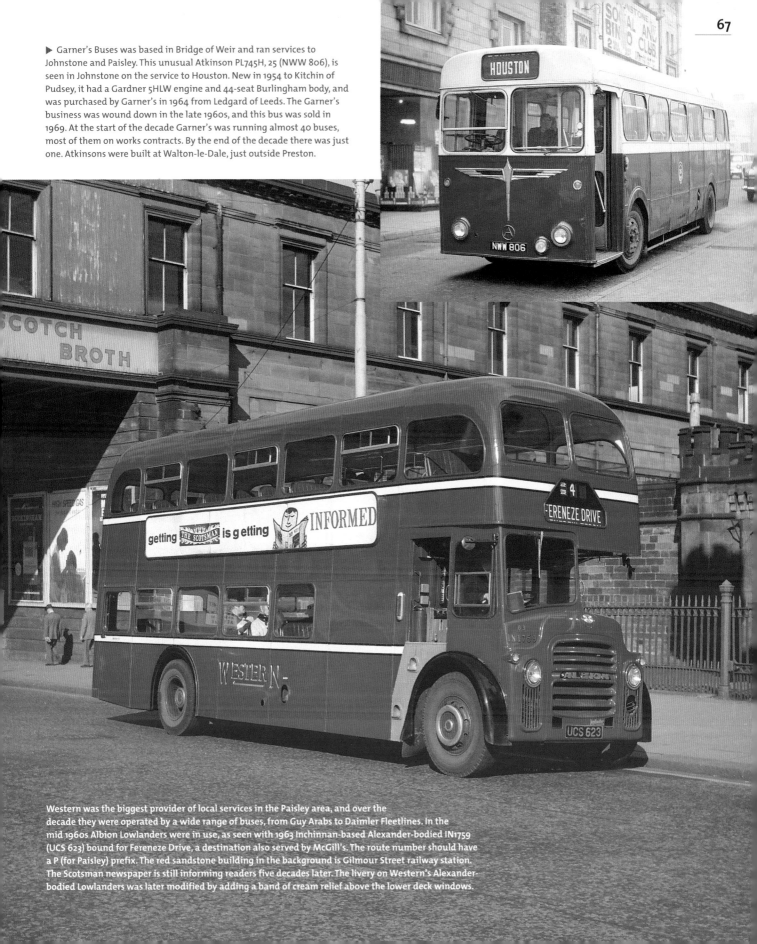

▶ Garner's Buses was based in Bridge of Weir and ran services to Johnstone and Paisley. This unusual Atkinson PL745H, 25 (NWW 806), is seen in Johnstone on the service to Houston. New in 1954 to Kitchin of Pudsey, it had a Gardner 5HLW engine and 44-seat Burlingham body, and was purchased by Garner's in 1964 from Ledgard of Leeds. The Garner's business was wound down in the late 1960s, and this bus was sold in 1969. At the start of the decade Garner's was running almost 40 buses, most of them on works contracts. By the end of the decade there was just one. Atkinsons were built at Walton-le-Dale, just outside Preston.

Western was the biggest provider of local services in the Paisley area, and over the decade they were operated by a wide range of buses, from Guy Arabs to Daimler Fleetlines. In the mid 1960s Albion Lowlanders were in use, as seen with 1963 Inchinnan-based Alexander-bodied IN1759 (UCS 623) bound for Fereneze Drive, a destination also served by McGill's. The route number should have a P (for Paisley) prefix. The red sandstone building in the background is Gilmour Street railway station. The Scotsman newspaper is still informing readers five decades later. The livery on Western's Alexander-bodied Lowlanders was later modified by adding a band of cream relief above the lower deck windows.

▶ McGill's was the first operator of a rear-engined bus in Paisley, with a Fleetline in the spring of 1963. There were eight in service by 1969, replacing Guy Arabs and Leyland Titans. The first Fleetline had a Northern Counties body, but subsequent deliveries were bodied by Alexander. Three were delivered in 1965. The conductress on CHS 722C chats to the driver as passengers board in Gilmour Street, Paisley.

▶ From the middle of the 1960s Paton adopted a brighter livery. It was inspired by this ex-St Helens Corporation Titan PD2, and copied that operator's layout. The bus is waiting in Caledonia Street, Paisley, for its departure time to Govan Cross and features another example of the lazy destination display, showing both of the route's terminal points at the same time. This PD2/20 with 61-seat East Lancs body was the first bus in the Paton fleet with a new-look front. It was also a relatively young purchase, being just ten years old when it was acquired by Paton in 1966; Paton at that time was typically buying Titans between 15 and 19 years old.

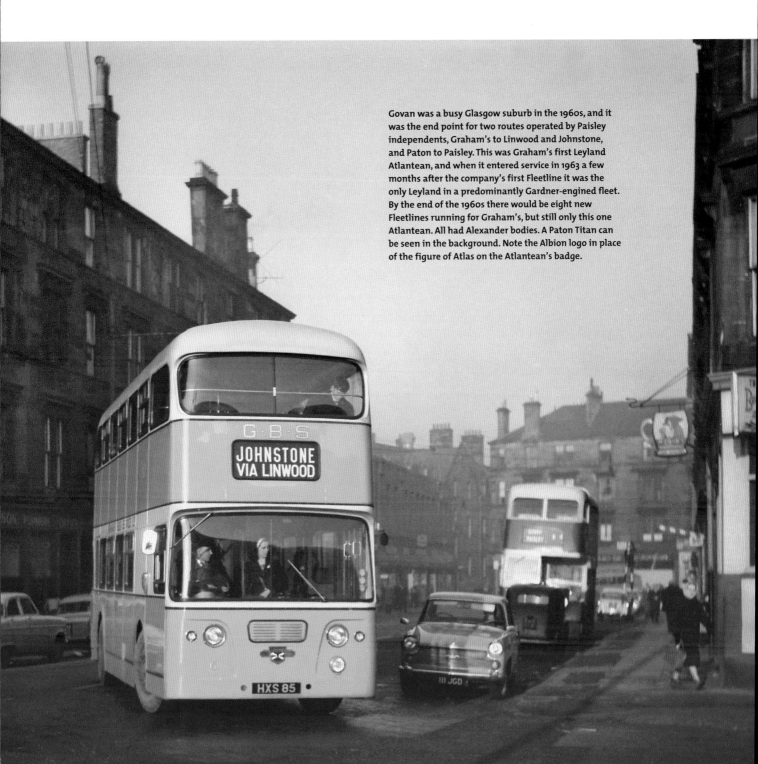

Govan was a busy Glasgow suburb in the 1960s, and it was the end point for two routes operated by Paisley independents, Graham's to Linwood and Johnstone, and Paton to Paisley. This was Graham's first Leyland Atlantean, and when it entered service in 1963 a few months after the company's first Fleetline it was the only Leyland in a predominantly Gardner-engined fleet. By the end of the 1960s there would be eight new Fleetlines running for Graham's, but still only this one Atlantean. All had Alexander bodies. A Paton Titan can be seen in the background. Note the Albion logo in place of the figure of Atlas on the Atlantean's badge.

Rear-engined single-deckers

Setting aside the somewhat idiosyncratic Albion Viking favoured by the Scottish Bus Group from 1965, rear-engined single-deckers were few and far between in 1960s Scotland. The first conventional rear-engined low-frame model for a Scottish operator was a Leyland Panther for Glasgow Corporation. This entered service in May 1965 and was the Corporation's first one-man-operated bus. It had been an exhibit at the Commercial Motor Show at London's Earls Court in September 1964. It was only the second Panther built, and like all Glasgow's Panthers had two-door Alexander W-type bodywork. A second followed in 1966, after being at the 1965 Scottish Motor Show. A third arrived in 1968 – Glasgow (wisely, as other operators' experiences would show) wasn't rushing in to one-man-operated Panthers – and it, too, was a Scottish Motor Show exhibit, in November 1967. It differed from the fleet's other Panthers in having panoramic windows. And then finally a batch of 13 (an inauspicious number) was delivered in 1969.

The next rear-engined model to appear in Scotland was the Daimler Roadliner SRC6 which, with its Cummins V6 engine and legendary unreliability, proved to be one of the bus industry's great disasters. An SRC6 with Plaxton bus body was delivered to Tumilty of Irvine in 1966, the only new Roadliner in Scotland.

Scotland's 1960s low-frame rear-engined buses	
AEC Swift	39
Bristol RELL6G	12
Daimler Roadliner	1
Leyland Panther	16
Total	68

▲ The first rear-engined single-deck bus to enter service in Scotland did so with Glasgow Corporation in May 1965. LS31 (CYS 139B) was one of the first Leyland Panther PSUR1/1 chassis to be built and had the first example of Alexander's W-type body. It had been an exhibit at the 1964 Commercial Motor Show at London's Earls Court. It was a dual-door 42-seater, and like all of Glasgow's Panthers carried a reversed version of the Corporation's yellow and green livery. It was Glasgow's first one-man-operated bus, and the panel above the destination advises: "Pay as you enter. One man operated bus." It initially operated from Newlands depot on suburban service 40, which linked Cathcart and Peat Road on the south side of the city, but after a few months – presumably during which the Corporation confirmed that the newfangled concept of one-man operation actually worked – it was transferred to a route running into the centre of the city. It would be withdrawn in 1971.

Tumilty was part of the AA co-operative and a long-standing Daimler operator, running new and second-hand CVD6s, a rare CD650 (one of just two in Scotland) and a Fleetline. The Roadliner was Tumilty's last new Daimler. The operator's next new bus, in 1968, was an ultra-reliable Leyland Leopard. The Roadliner would be scrapped in 1973, despite an attempt to extend its life by fitting a Perkins V8 engine.

In the summer of 1968 Alexander Fife received 12 Bristol RELL6Gs with 53-seat ECW bodies, SBG's first low-floor (by 1960s standards) single-deckers. Although these constituted a relatively small batch of non-standard buses, they were shared between five different depots when new.

Scotland's first AEC Swifts entered service in 1968. Aberdeen Corporation received ten with 43-seat two-door Alexander W-type bodies, and these were used to expand one-man-operation in a fleet made up mainly of double-deckers. A further 15 followed in 1969, and more would be purchased in the 1970s.

More unusual 1968 Swift deliveries were four to Hutchison of Overtown. Hutchison's bus fleet at this time was composed entirely of AEC Reliances, and from 1965 all of the company's new Reliances buses had been 36ft-long Willowbrook 53-seaters. Two of the Swifts had Willowbrook bodies, which was the logical choice in the light of Hutchison's relationship with the Loughborough bodybuilder, but the other two were bodied by Alexander. A further seven Willowbrook-bodied Swifts were ordered by Hutchison, but were cancelled before they were built.

The final 1960s rear-engined single-deckers were also Swifts, ten with 43-seat Alexander W-type bodies for Dundee. Here, as in Aberdeen, the fleet was predominantly double-decked and the Swifts were being used to extend one-man-operation. In 1968 Dundee ordered 25 Fleetline single-deckers, giving standardisation with its double-deck fleet, but these would not be delivered until 1970. ∎

The Alexander W-type was also offered with panoramic windows, and this was the choice made by Aberdeen Corporation for 25 AEC Swifts in 1968 and 1969, and for follow-on deliveries in the 1970s. They were two-door 43-seaters. Note the different headlight arrangement compared with the Glasgow bus. 23 (JRS 23F) was one of ten delivered in 1968 and is seen soon after delivery loading in Castle Street. The use of lower case lettering for the destination was unusual.

The Highlands

The Scottish Highlands were not good bus
territory. Inverness was the only substantial
town – population 30,000 – and in the early
1960s there were only two other towns in the region
with a population in excess of 5,000, Nairn and Wick.
There were also significant distances between the
centres of population, and a road network characterised
by long stretches of single track roads with passing
places marked by a white diamond atop a striped pole.

This sparsely-populated region was served in the
1960s by two major operators, MacBrayne and Highland

▲ ▶ There often seemed little logic in the selection of vehicles
to be transferred to Highland from other SBG companies, and
six Daimler CVD6s from Alexander Midland seemed an odd
choice in 1965, considering that Highland had no Daimler-
engined buses. Four had Burlingham half-cab bodies and two
were 30ft-long models with fully-fronted 37-seat ECW bodies.
The Daimlers created a new DA class at Highland (D was
in use for Daimler double-deckers). Freshly-painted DA6
(DMS 561) heads for Balloch, while DA2 (BMS 402) waits to
take up a trip to Nairn via Culloden. All had gone by 1967.
The heavy manually-operated sliding door made these
coaches less than ideal for local bus operation.

Omnibuses, and by a number of smaller businesses, most of whom gave up as the decade progressed. Between 1964 and 1969 Highland Omnibuses took over the services of 11 small operators, only two of which ran more than six vehicles. Highland Omnibuses was a relatively young company in 1960, having been created in 1952 to take over the businesses of Highland Transport (69 buses) and Macrae & Dick (25 vehicles), along with the Inverness operations of Alexander (24 buses).

MacBrayne and Highland had quite different vehicle policies. The former bought new buses and coaches, and in the 1960s these were AECs and Bedfords. The only second-hand vehicles in its 118-strong fleet in 1960 were two acquired with the business of Skye Transport in 1958. The picture at Highland Omnibuses was completely different. In 1960 Highland was running 145 vehicles of which 50 were second-hand – counting as new the vehicles acquired from its predecessor companies. In the ensuing ten years Highland added 315 buses and coaches to its fleet (excluding those which came from acquired business), and of these

HIGHLAND OMNIBUSES

Highland Coach Tours

SEASON 1961

◀ At the start of the decade the cover of Highland's coach tour brochure featured an ex-Scottish Omnibuses Burlingham-bodied Bedford SB. New in 1952, C31 (JSF 831) had joined the Highland fleet in 1959.

▼ This MacBrayne advert from the start of the decade shows two Duple-bodied Bedford SBGs awaiting the arrival of steamer King George V at Fort William.

MISCELLANEOUS ADVERTISEMENTS

See Scotland's lovely Western Highlands and Islands this year

MacBrayne's modern vessels and coaches cover many enchanting routes in the Western Highlands and Islands. There is a constant panorama of beauty and the countryside and islands are steeped in history, legend and romance.

MACBRAYNES

Write for Brochure P1 giving details of services and tours to:

DAVID MACBRAYNE LTD, CLYDE HOUSE, 44 ROBERTSON ST, GLASGOW C2

Please mention this Guide when replying to Advertisers.

▼ In the 1940s MacBrayne had been Scotland's biggest buyer of Maudslays, taking 34 Marathon IIIs between 1947 and 1949, all but one of which were still in service in 1960. Most of the Maudslays had old-fashioned-looking Park Royal bodies, as seen on this 1949 coach outside the company's Fort William depot. 136 (GUS 926) was withdrawn in 1966, by which time it was the sole survivor with its original body. The last of four rebodied Marathons survived only two years longer, being withdrawn in 1968.

250 were second-hand, mainly from other SBG companies, and just 65 were new. The upshot of all this was that by 1969 Highland was running 240 buses, of which 150 were second-hand. Thus the proportion of second-hand buses in the fleet almost doubled in the decade from 34 to 63 per cent.

Some of Highland's administration was handled from Edinburgh by Scottish Omnibuses. A visible sign of this was Highland's use of the same prefix letters for some of its fleet numbers as were used by SOL (eg B for AECs, C for Bedfords), although this changed during the 1960s. The company's choice of new AECs in the 1950s and early 1960s also echoed Scottish Omnibuses' policy, as did the layout of its single-deck bus livery with a cream waistband and roof.

Highland Omnibuses' territory stretched from Nairn on the Moray Firth, through Inverness and then north to Wick, Thurso and John o'Groats. A measure of the size of Highland's operating area is that the trunk service from Inverness to Wick covered a distance of almost 150 miles. Although shown in timetables as a through service, on most journeys there were lengthy breaks at Dornoch and Helmsdale which meant the end-to-end journey

▲ In 1963 this was the most modern double-decker in the Highland fleet, a Guy Arab III with 57-seat lowbridge Strachans body which had entered service in 1951 after being exhibited at the 1950 Commercial Motor Show. Highland Transport was a big Strachans customer after the war, taking single- and double-deck bodies on 18 Arabs between 1946 and 1951. E72 (EST 392) was withdrawn by Highland Omnibuses in 1970, at which time it was the last ex-Highland Transport vehicle in the fleet. Fully-fronted double-deckers were rare in Scotland; there were only three others in the 1960s, one each at AA, A1 and Garelochhead Coach Services.

▶ Throughout the 1960s most of Highland's buses were redundant vehicles transferred from sister SBG companies. Nearest the camera is E42 (EFS 357) a 1945 Weymann-bodied Guy Arab II. It was one of 17 transferred from Scottish Omnibuses in the 1950s, the last of which were withdrawn by Highland in 1967. Alongside is ex-Western SMT Alexander-bodied Daimler CVG6 D4 (BSD 292). Three of these operated in the Highland fleet for nine months in 1964–65, retaining Western livery and on this bus even using Western transfers for the Highland fleet numbers. They had been new in 1951. The location of this and many other pictures on these pages is Highland's bus station in Farraline Park, Inverness.

▼ Consecutive registrations, contrasting style. The last new half-cab single-deckers for a Scottish operator were three AEC Regal IIIs with 35-seat Roe bodies, which were delivered to MacBrayne in 1953 along with two Roe-bodied Regal IVs. Two of the Regal IIIs were fitted with new Duple coach bodies in 1961, as shown by 27 (KGG 709) on the right. 30 (KGG 710), which retained its original body, was withdrawn in 1966; the rebodied coaches lasted until 1969 and 1970. The Regals are seen on the pier at Fort William on a dreich summer day.

▼ ▶ Between 1957 and 1962 Highland received 39 new AEC Reliances and Monocoaches. The final 12, in 1961–62, were Reliances with 38-seat Alexander coach bodies based on the manufacturer's standard dual-purpose body shell but with glazed cove panels, glazing in the front dome, stylish side mouldings, twin destination screens below the windscreen and a single-piece inswing door. The result was a surprisingly attractive transformation of a standard SBG workhorse, as illustrated by B40 (SST 996). From 1966 these coaches were repainted in Highland's new blue and grey coach livery. The standard version of the Alexander body is illustrated by B25 (OST 503) of 1960. A plate in the nearside windscreen reads "On hire to BEA". British European Airways held the licence for the service between Inverness and the airport at Dalcross, with Highland providing the vehicles. The "On hire" notice was a legal requirement when a vehicle was running on a service which was licensed to another operator.

time was typically 10½ hours, an average of 15mph. The quickest through journey in 1965 was 8¾ hours. The best bet for through travellers was to forget the bus and take the train, which typically made the trip in 4½ hours.

Timetable oddities at Highland in the middle of the decade saw not just rural services which only operated one or two days a week, but the winter service between Laide and Inverness which operated on alternate Thursdays, and town services in Wick and Thurso which offered four round trips on weekdays except on early closing day when there was no afternoon service.

MacBrayne's territory was generally to the south and west of the Great Glen, and the biggest town in which it was the major operator was Fort William. In the 1960s all of Highland Omnibuses' services were on the mainland. By contrast MacBrayne served a number of islands including Islay, Mull and Skye. Many MacBrayne buses were equipped with large mail and goods compartments, with access through doors on the rear of the body. ∎

▲ There was a major improvement in Highland's double-deck fleet in 1963 with the arrival of 12 Bristol Lodekkas from Scottish Omnibuses, which repainted them before dispatching them north. They were seven years old and were used mainly on Inverness town services. They were numbered L1-12 (L for Lodekka) and replaced ageing Guy Arabs. L9 (NSG 788) leaves Farraline Park for Drummond School in 1965. Scottish Omnibuses was often short of buses and the Highland-liveried Lodekkas saw brief service in Edinburgh in the summer of 1963 before being dispatched north. Even more surprising, the elderly Guys they were replacing were used in Edinburgh for a few months before finally being withdrawn.

◀ Alexander Northern also operated Reliances on services to Inverness, and here one leaves for Macduff on a short-working of the service to Aberdeen via the coast. "Short working" is perhaps a misnomer for a journey taking 3½ hours; the end-to-end trip from Inverness to Aberdeen took 5½ hours. Vehicles in the Northern fleet with this style of body always wore coach rather than bus livery, even at the end of their lives. NAC200 (RMS 734) was delivered in May 1961 just as the Alexander business was being split into three.

◀ ▼ This ex-Western Arab UF in the Highland fleet, K22 (FAG 92), had a unique style of Alexander body, based on that in the bottom left photograph but with different glazing and side mouldings, and with a sliding instead of a folding door. It had been a Guy exhibit at the 1952 Commercial Motor Show and was purchased by Western the following year. It joined the Highland fleet in 1965, originally running in coach livery before being repainted in a scheme with more red. The mouldings around the front were simplified when it was repainted. In coach livery it is ready for the 3½ hour journey to Dornoch; as a bus it is heading to Nairn, a more modest one-hour trip.

▼ Western SMT operated 36 Guy Arab UFs with centre-entrance Alexander bodies, delivered in 1952–53. All were acquired by Highland between 1963 and 1965, initially running in coach livery as seen here, but later being repainted predominantly red. Most ran for four or five years with Highland, the last being withdrawn in 1970. As with many Highland buses in the 1960s K8 (EAG 898), headed for Nairn, relies on a paper sticker in the windscreen rather than a proper destination display. You would need sharp eyes to read the small print – "via Culloden" – under the word Nairn.

HIGHLAND
DOUNREAY

GYL 421

Was this the most northerly ex-London Transport bus? Highland E30 (GYL 421) was a Northern Counties-bodied Arab II which had been new to LT as G281 in 1945. It was purchased by Western SMT in 1953, and was transferred to Highland in 1957, where it operated until 1966. It is seen at Dounreay, where there was a United Kingdom Atomic Energy Authority site which was served by over two dozen Highland buses. These brought workers in in the morning and were then parked all day before returning the workers home in the evening.

▲ John o'Groats is not quite the most northerly point on the British mainland, but it's where the tourists go. Highland CD9 (JJS 17) is a Bedford SB1 with 41-seat Duple Super Vega body. It had been new in 1961 to MacKenzie of Garve, whose business was taken over by Highland in the autumn of 1964. The blue and grey coach livery had been adopted in 1966 and was inspired by a second-hand Thames purchased from Happiways Tours of Manchester. This coach would operate for Highland until 1976.

▼ The Sutherland Transport & Trading Company operated a number of lengthy routes between Lairg and communities in the far north and west, generally using small Bedfords. ANS 517C was a 1965 Bedford VAS1 with bodywork by Bedford dealer SMT Sales & Service of Edinburgh. It had just 16 seats – a VAS bus typically seated 30 – with the rear of the body being occupied by a large compartment for mail and goods. It was the last of four generally similar buses bought by the company in the 1960s. Sutherland Transport's services were centred on Lairg Post Office, the location of this view. Buses ran in to the town from outlying villages in the morning and returned in the afternoon, connecting with trains from the south which were carrying mail; note the Royal Mail lettering on the side of the goods compartment.

◀ Robertson of Strathglass ran a service between Tomich and Beauly, and from 1963 to 1967 used this 1955 petrol-engined Bedford SBG with bodywork by Thurgood of Ware. The Robertson business was purchased by Highland in 1967, and this coach, UNK 229, briefly became the only Thurgood-bodied vehicle to be operated by the Scottish Bus Group. It is seen in Beauly. The grille is made up of parts from the mid-1950s Humber Hawk car.

◀ There was one substantial independent operator in Moray, Smith of Grantown-on-Spey. The company had 16 vehicles and served the Cairngorm ski slopes. It ran a motley collection of second-hand buses, one of the more unusual being this 1950 Albion Victor FT39N with 32-seat Alexander body, DRS 666, which had been new to Simpson's Heatherbell Coach Tours of Aberdeen. Only two bodies of this style were built by Alexander. This Victor was in the Smith fleet when the business was purchased by Highland in December 1966 but was sold by Highland without being used. It is seen in Newtonmore on Smith's service from Grantown.

▼ In sharp contrast to Highland Omnibuses with its eclectic collection of elderly second-hand buses, MacBrayne bought new vehicles, and from 1958 standardised on the AEC Reliance for its full-size buses and coaches. Until 1962 most were specified with Duple Donington bodies. 53 (294 AGE) is a 1960 coach and was one of the first Scottish PSVs with a reversed registration; it is seen on the quayside at Tarbert. Ultimately there were 20 Doningtons in the MacBrayne fleet, and they replaced Maudslay Marathons and AEC Regals. Later Doningtons had fewer, bigger, side windows.

▼ Both of the major Highlands operators bought new Bedford coaches in 1967, but of rather different styles. MacBrayne took four SB5s with 41-seat Plaxton Embassy bodies, including 168 (MGB 286E). These were the company's first new Plaxton coaches and were 7ft 6in wide. Another eight would follow by 1970. Highland's 1967 Bedfords were six VAM5s with Alexander Y-type bodies seating 38 or 41. This is CD19 (EST 823E). Highland's original Bedford coaches were petrol-engined and had been given the same C classification as was used for Bedfords by Scottish Omnibuses. The CD class letters indicated a Diesel-engined Bedford. The coaches were photographed in Fort William in the spring of 1968.

The Clyde

In the 1960s many bus enthusiasts were attracted to what were known as the Ayrshire independents – A1, AA and Clyde Coast – which ran services in overlapping territory on the Ayrshire coast, stretching 35 miles from Largs in the north to Ayr in the south, and inland as far as Kilmarnock. These three were unusual in being co-operatives with individual members owning the buses, but operating under a common trading name which presented a unified image to passengers.

Clyde Coast, with four members in the early 1960s, was the smallest, with one trunk route from Largs to Saltcoats. This met the operating areas of AA and A1 at Ardrossan. AA's principal route ran

▲ Operation on the Clyde coast is typified by this scene in the resort town of Largs. This was the most northerly town served by Ayrshire's main independent operators, with Clyde Coast's service running south to Saltcoats. When Barrow Corporation withdrew its fleet of 20 Crossley DD42s after just ten years in service, a number were snapped up by Scottish operators, with five going to Clyde Coast, three to Graham's of Paisley and one to A1. They had Crossley bodies with that manufacturer's distinctive stepped waistline. The longest-lived of Clyde Coast's Crossleys ran until 1967 when they were replaced by ex-Trent Leyland Titans. EO 8789 was new in 1948.

from Ardrossan to Ayr – the source of the AA name – but it had other services too, including local routes in Troon and Ayr. There were three members in the AA co-operative. A1 was the biggest of the three Ayrshire co-operatives, with 16 members owning 70 vehicles, and its trunk service ran from Ardrossan to Irvine, and then inland to Kilmarnock, but it too had other local routes, notably around Irvine and Stevenston.

Overlaid across these independents' services was the Western SMT network. This included services from the main coastal towns to Glasgow, along with other interurban routes and local services in Ayr and Kilmarnock. The company had three major depots in Ayrshire, at Ardrossan (50 buses), Ayr (130) and Kilmarnock (150).

Expanding the Clyde coastal area beyond Ayrshire, there was a Western depot in Greenock, Renfrewshire, where 150 buses ran a

▲ Helensburgh was a popular resort on the north bank of the Clyde. The town's Central station was the terminus for Garelochhead Coach Services' eight-mile route to the small town from which the company took its name. In the 1960s the service was normally operated by AEC Regent Vs. 28 (JSN 584) is a 1959 bus with 65-seat Alexander body, one of two similar vehicles. It is heading to Garelochhead, passing the Commodore Hotel on Helensburgh sea front. Garelochhead Coach Services would buy Scotland's last new Regent (and last new half-cab bus) in 1968 by which time the company would have purchased six new Regent Vs.

Most of Garelochhead's buses in the 1960s were second-hand, and included ex-London Transport RFs, RTs and RTLs, one of which was 47 (KXW 4), new in 1950 as London RTL654. It had a Metro-Cammell body. It was purchased by Garelochhead in 1965 and is laying over in Colquhoun Square in Helensburgh, where the company operated a local service.

▶ The most unusual bus in the 1960s Garelochhead fleet was this Foden PVD6, 13 (JGD 675), seen on a contract in Dumbarton. Built in 1948 but not registered until 1951, it was the first double-decker to be produced by Scottish Aviation of Prestwick. It was registered in Glasgow by Foy, who formed the Garelochhead business in 1951 after taking over from the previous operator, Brown. Only eight Foden double-deckers operated in Scotland, and when JGD 675 was withdrawn in 1968 it was the last survivor.

local network in the linked towns of Port Glasgow, Greenock and Gourock, as well as operating longer-distance routes west to Glasgow and south to Largs, Irvine and Kilmarnock.

On the opposite bank of the river the resort town of Helensburgh in Dunbartonshire was the starting point of the main service operated by Garelochhead Coach Services, running north-west along the edge of the Clyde and the Garelochh to the company's base in Garelochhead. Helensburgh was also served by Central SMT

Central's Old Kilpatrick depot operated services from Glasgow to Balloch. Central's Balloch services were unusual for a company serving predominantly industrial areas in having different winter and summer timetables. The Sunday afternoon services were increased in frequency from 7½ minutes in the winter to 6 minutes in the summer to cater for Glaswegians visiting Loch Lomond. This is a winter view of 1948 Leyland Titan PD2 L352 (DVD 210) with 53-seat Leyland lowbridge body. It was part of a batch of 100, the biggest single double-deck bus order placed by an SMT group company.

▲ Services between Glasgow and Helensburgh were provided by Central SMT using Leyland Titan PD2s based at its Old Kilpatrick depot. L597 (GM 9957) is a 1959 PD2/30 with 59-seat Northern Counties body. Central was the only SBG company to specify a side destination display, visible above the rear platform.

◀ Helensburgh was a popular destination for coach trips. Midland Leyland Tiger Cub PD208 (RMS 697) from Stirling depot has stopped in the town while on a Three Lochs tour. There were 20 Tiger Cubs with this style of body, delivered in 1961. The structure was that of the standard Alexander dual-purpose coach, complete with short centre bay, but its appearance was transformed with stylish glass fibre mouldings for the front and rear ends, glazed cove panels, new side mouldings and a one-piece inswing door. The coach behind is a Duple-bodied Bedford SB operated by Browning of Whitburn.

Also on a day trip to Helensburgh is Eastern Scottish AEC Reliance B677H (SWS 677) with 38-seat Alexander body, freshly repainted in the Lothian green dual-purpose livery adopted in 1965. There were 20 coaches in this batch which when new were commonly referred to as the "two-day Reliances" because they were used primarily on SOL's two-day tourist service between Edinburgh and London. The body differed from the standard Alexander product in a number of details, including glazing in the cove panels and front dome, and in the absence of the characteristic short centre bay for the emergency exit.

Dunoon Motor Services ran assorted double-deckers in the early 1960s including ex-Glasgow Corporation and ex-Western SMT Albion Venturers, and Leyland Titans from Ribble and, as here, Wallasey Corporation. AHF 198 is a 1948 Leyland Titan PD1 with a remarkably old-fashioned-looking Metro-Cammell body. It was purchased from Tiger Coaches, the Salsburgh dealer and vehicle dismantler. It is heading for Toward Castle – pronounced to rhyme with "coward", although strangers could read the destination as "toward castle". Dunoon's illuminations, strung above the bus, look to be no match for Blackpool's.

▶ In 1965 the local services in Dunoon were taken over by a new operator, Cowal Motor Services. Out went the old buses of Dunoon Motor Services, replaced by six four-year-old Thames 570Es with Duple Yeoman 41-seat coach bodies. They came from Trimdon Motor Services. A bill in the windscreen shows 860 JPT is on the Sandbank service.

which operated to Glasgow, but which was facing competition with the new Blue Train electric service inaugurated in 1960 to replace steam-hauled trains. Central had a depot at Old Kilpatrick, roughly midway between Helensburgh and Glasgow, and its operations included town services in Dumbarton and routes between Glasgow and Balloch on the edge of Loch Lomond. The services operated from Old Kilpatrick, which had an allocation of 120 buses, were not connected with the rest of Central SMT's operations in Lanarkshire.

Dunoon was the largest Clyde coast town not to be served by the Scottish Bus Group. By dint of its geography, the easiest way of getting from Dunoon to Glasgow or other central belt towns was by ferry to Gourock, making the onward journey by train or Western SMT bus. Local services in the town were at the start of the 1960s provided by Dunoon Motor Services with a collection of elderly second-hand buses. That changed in 1965 when Cowal Motor Services took over, initially with modern second-hand coaches.

The other principal bus operations on the Clyde were mainly on islands. Western SMT served Bute with 28 buses and coaches.

▲ Services on Bute were operated by Western SMT which had 28 vehicles based on the island, housed in the former Rothesay Tramways depot at Port Bannatyne. In the mid 1960s the Bute fleet included 14 Bristol MW6Gs with 41-seat Alexander bodies, a chassis/body combination unique to Western. RT1283 (JSD 919) carries the code A7 above the fleet number, indicating a vehicle new in 1957. The year code had been introduced in 1965. It would be abandoned at the end of the 1970s.

▼ Great Cumbrae is a small island, just 2½ miles from end to end. There is only one town, Millport, which in the 1960s had a population of 2,000, although this would rise substantially in the summer months with holiday visitors arriving on the Caledonian Steam Packet Company's service from Largs. Millport Motors was the island's bus operator and in 1964 it was running this 1950 Albion Victor FT39N with 31-seat Scottish Aviation body, DAG 983, which had been new to Paterson of Dalry. Instead of a fleetname the lettering on the side reads "Tours round the island", while the destination screen offers the less inviting option of "Keppel Pier via housing scheme".

▼ Rothesay's double-deckers were usually Leyland Titans. AD2182 (XS 6909) is a highbridge PD2 with Leyland body which had been new in 1950 to Young's Bus Service of Paisley. The Ayr depot code suggests it was either on loan or had only recently been transferred when photographed leaving for Ettrick Bay. An intriguing feature on the last Sunday night trip on this and some other Bute services was the enigmatic note in the timetable: "Waits entertainers".

The return of Strachans to double-deck bus building saw the Hamble-based company win orders for five bodies from Scottish operators in 1962–63. Four of these were for A1, three on Regent Vs plus one on a Leyland Titan PD2A/30 chassis. The Titan, WCS 197, was owned by Docherty of Irvine and is seen in A1's basic bus terminal in Parkhouse Road, Ardrossan, alongside Regent WCS 195 which was owned by Hill of Stevenston. Both were 63-seaters. Strachan's fifth Scottish order was the Guy Arab for Graham's illustrated on page 66.

Until 1965 McGill's of Barrhead had a small subsidiary on the island, Rothesay Motor Services, running day tours and a circular service to Canada Hill. On Cumbrae, the operator was Millport Motors. The biggest of the islands was Arran, and this had six small operators at the start of the decade – but one dominant operator, Arran Transport, and one smaller operator, Bannatyne, by the end.

That rationalisation might be coming for bus operators on Arran was foreshadowed in a report in the Glasgow *Evening Times* in 1963 noting that the introduction of car ferries by the Caledonian Steam Packet Co meant that more visitors to the island were bringing their cars. Veteran reporter Jack House wrote: "You have so many people coming over in their cars that the bus operators on the island are seriously worried. One chap told me that the number of cars landed on Arran during last holiday season was 14,000. That's bad enough but what makes it worse from the 'Round Arran' bus point of view, is that a couple with a car will invite a carless couple in the same hotel to tour the island with them. So that's two customers lost to the bus." Or, perhaps, four.

The most remote of the Firth of Clyde towns was Campbeltown. From Glasgow it was around 140 miles by road – the MacBrayne service took almost six hours. There were two independents based in the town, West Coast Motor Services and McConnachie. The later operated Kintyre's only double-deckers, and was taken over by West Coast in 1969. ■

◀ AA member Young of Ayr bought three Leyland Atlanteans which had Northern Counties bodies with unusual Nottingham-style fronts. A translucent panel in the roof sheds extra light on the staircase. EAG 267D, new in 1966, was the second of these Atlanteans and is seen turning into Glasgow Street, Ardrossan, on its way to Ayr.

▼ A rather different Leyland owned by Young in 1966 was this ex-Ribble Leyland Titan PD2, CCK 343, new in 1948. It joined the AA fleet in 1962, and was operated for five years. It is in Irvine on the service to Stevenston, outside the premises of the Unionist Club where a poster in the upstairs window warns: "The cost of socialism is going up every day" and urges people to join the Conservatives.

◀ The small rectangular windscreen made Northern Coachbuilders bodies on Daimler CVD6 chassis look a bit old-fashioned, as demonstrated by an AA bus owned by Tumilty of Irvine. New in 1948 to Sheffield, KWB 914 was operated by AA from 1960 to 1966, and is seen in Irvine shortly before being withdrawn. Tumilty favoured Daimlers and in the early 1960s was operating eight, bought both new and used. Similar Northern Coachbuilders-bodied Daimlers were bought by three of Scotland's municipal fleets, Aberdeen, which had 25, and Glasgow and Dundee which each had 20. A 1960 Humber Hawk is parked at the kerb.

◀ Millburn Motors, the Glasgow-based Leyland dealer, had two Titan PD3s built for stock in 1962. They had 72-seat Alexander bodies similar to a batch being supplied to Glasgow Corporation. The only significant difference from the Glasgow buses was the use of red rather than green for the interior finish. One was sold to Carmichael of Glenboig, for operation on a new town service in Cumbernauld, while the other went to A1 member Docherty of Irvine. TSD 285 passes Irvine Cross on its way to Kilmarnock, followed by a Western SMT Lowlander. The Titan's registration would later be transferred to an A1 Volvo Citybus.

▶ Western SMT was the major operator in Ayr, where it had a depot with an allocation of 130 vehicles. Particularly striking coaches in the fleet at the start of the 1960s were its Alexander-bodied Guy Arab UFs. There were 36, new in 1952-53, all but one with this style of body. Most spent their early years on the Glasgow to London service, and all were transferred to Highland Omnibuses between 1963 and 1965. Similar coaches were supplied to Central SMT and, on Leyland Royal Tiger chassis, to Alexander. Western Arab AG958 (EAG 460) is seen in Ayr bus station. These were heavy coaches by the standards of the day, weighing just under 8 tons unladen.

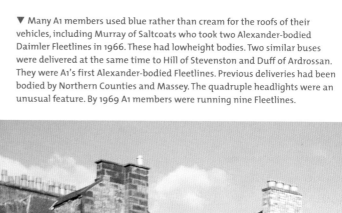

▼ Many A1 members used blue rather than cream for the roofs of their vehicles, including Murray of Saltcoats who took two Alexander-bodied Daimler Fleetlines in 1966. These had lowheight bodies. Two similar buses were delivered at the same time to Hill of Stevenston and Duff of Ardrossan. They were A1's first Alexander-bodied Fleetlines. Previous deliveries had been bodied by Northern Counties and Massey. The quadruple headlights were an unusual feature. By 1969 A1 members were running nine Fleetlines.

▲ AA operated local services in Irvine, as seen here with Tumilty Daimler CVG6 KAG 573 headed for Rubie Crescent. The bus was new in 1957 and had an Alexander body with 63 seats and rear platform doors. The combination of the curved roof profile of the Alexander body and the Birmingham-style new-look front created a particularly attractive bus.

▼ Well-loaded Western Leyland Titan MD492 (BCS 342) of Newton Mearns depot leaves Ayr for Glasgow on a summer evening in 1964. Western had 45 of these Leyland-bodied PD1s, delivered in 1947. They served the company well, with some running until 1967. The company's tours office is visible on the left. The advert on the bus declares: "It's an old Scottish custom – to open a credit account with Dan Flynn (Bookmakers) Ltd".

Five AEC Renowns were supplied new to Scottish operators, one for Scottish Omnibuses and two each for Smith of Barrhead and A1. The A1 buses were owned by McKinnon of Kilmarnock and had 75-seat Park Royal bodies. They entered service in 1964. ASD 890B approaches the A1 bus station in Kilmarnock. A 1962 Standard Atlas van is parked in the background.

▶ AA had its own bus station in Ayr, a short distance from Western's terminal. Dodds Guy Arab DT No12 (CSD 843) waits to depart for Annbank. Dodds bought three of these Arabs with Gardner 6LW engines and 56-seat Park Royal bodies in 1948–49. All three were rebuilt or rebodied in the 1960s and generally served Dodds for 20 years. The external ribs on the roof were a distinctive feature of this style of Park Royal body.

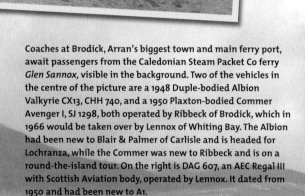

Coaches at Brodick, Arran's biggest town and main ferry port, await passengers from the Caledonian Steam Packet Co ferry *Glen Sannox*, visible in the background. Two of the vehicles in the centre of the picture are a 1948 Duple-bodied Albion Valkyrie CX13, CHH 740, and a 1950 Plaxton-bodied Commer Avenger I, SJ 1298, both operated by Ribbeck of Brodick, which in 1966 would be taken over by Lennox of Whiting Bay. The Albion had been new to Blair & Palmer of Carlisle and is headed for Lochranza, while the Commer was new to Ribbeck and is on a round-the-island tour. On the right is DAG 607, an AEC Regal III with Scottish Aviation body, operated by Lennox. It dated from 1950 and had been new to A1.

▲ There were 57 Northern Counties-bodied AEC Regent IIIs in the Western fleet in 1960. They were new between 1947 and 1950 and were withdrawn between 1962 and 1965. CC473 (BSD 436) of Cumnock depot speeds in to Ayr shortly before withdrawal in 1965. Similar bodywork was supplied to Western on 30 Regent II, 22 Daimler CVA6 and nine Leyland Titan PD1 chassis and was also used to rebody 22 prewar Titans and one wartime Guy to give the company a total of 141 bodies of this style.

▼ The Daimler CD650 was another rarity with just 14 sold in the UK. The CD650 had a 150bhp 10.6-litre Daimler engine, instead of the 100bhp 8.6-litre unit used in the contemporary CVD6. There were two CD650s in Scotland, one with Glasgow Corporation, which was withdrawn in 1960 after just nine years in service, and the other with AA member Tumilty. The chassis of Tumilty's bus was built around 1950 but was retained for testing by Daimler. It was purchased by Tumilty in 1954 and sent to Northern Counties where it was fitted with this 57-seat body and registered GAG 970. It ran for AA until 1972.

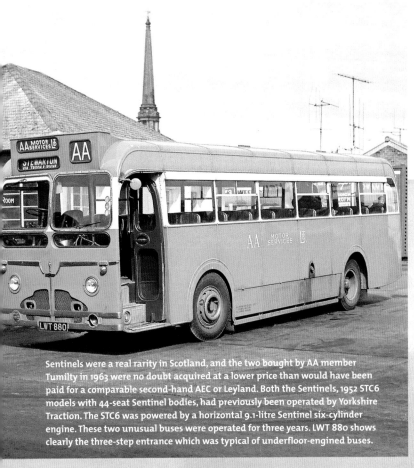

Sentinels were a real rarity in Scotland, and the two bought by AA member Tumilty in 1963 were no doubt acquired at a lower price than would have been paid for a comparable second-hand AEC or Leyland. Both the Sentinels, 1952 STC6 models with 44-seat Sentinel bodies, had previously been operated by Yorkshire Traction. The STC6 was powered by a horizontal 9.1-litre Sentinel six-cylinder engine. These two unusual buses were operated for three years. LWT 880 shows clearly the three-step entrance which was typical of underfloor-engined buses.

▶ Tumilty had a penchant for the unusual. This 1962-registered Daimler CVD6, TCS 402, was a rebuild based on a 1950 coach chassis which had originally carried a 7ft 6in-wide Plaxton body. Modifications included new axles for the 8ft-wide 63-seat Northern Counties body. It was fitted with a Gardner 6LW engine in 1967, making it a CVG6, and was withdrawn in 1971.

▼ Commers were a moderately popular alternative to the familiar Bedford OB, and around 100 were delivered to Scottish operators in the late 1940s. SJ 1189 with Plaxton body is seen with Ribbeck of Brodick. Commer coaches and lorries used the same 4.08-litre petrol engine as was fitted to Humber cars. Ribbeck's coaches carried a bluebird on the side.

▼ This Foden PVSC6 was built as a demonstrator by Scottish Aviation in 1948 and was sold to A1 member Hunter of Dreghorn at the end of that year. It ended its days on Arran, running for Bannatyne of Blackwaterfoot. It was one of just three Fodens to be fitted with Scottish Aviation coach bodies.

◀ West Coast Motor Services of Campbeltown operated this smart Bedford SB1 with Duple Super Vega body. GSB 571 had been new in 1961 to Gold Line of Dunoon and is seen on a private hire. West Coast was a regular buyer of Bedfords from Gold Line.

▶ The first double-decker on the Kintyre peninsula was KOD 585, a 1949 Weymann-bodied AEC Regent III which McConnachie bought from Devon General. Here it leaves Campbeltown for Machrihanish, five miles distant on the west coast. This bus survives, restored in Devon General livery.

Towards the end of the 1950s McConnachie of Campbeltown bought a pair of 10-year-old AEC Regal IIIs from Halifax Corporation. These had rear-entrance Roe bodies and were used primarily on town services. BCP 535 pulls out of the McConnachie depot. What had been the route number display is being used to show intermediate destinations Calton, High St, Meadows, with the main destination reading "Local via".

The revolutionary Y-type

The Alexander Y-type was a remarkable leap forward in coach and bus design. In the 1950s Alexander built a multiplicity of different styles of single-deck bus and coach bodies. The Y-type changed that. One body shell, with different window layouts, could serve as a bus or a coach. It was unveiled at the 1961 Scottish Motor Show with two striking vehicles which ably illustrated the versatility of the new body. Both were 36ft long. One was a three-door 33-seat standee bus on a Leyland Leopard chassis for Edinburgh Corporation, while the other was a panoramic-windowed 38-seat toilet-equipped luxury coach for use by Scottish Omnibuses on its prestigious Edinburgh to London express service. With a scheduled journey time of 14 hours and with 12 intermediate timing points it might not seem much like an express to modern travellers. (Today's day service between the two capital cities takes 10 hours with six stops, the night service 8 hours 35 minutes.)

The Alexander Y-type would prove to be one of the most significant models in Scottish bus history. Most early Y-types were 41- or 49-seat coaches with panoramic windows, but SBG companies saw the 36ft-long multi-windowed bus version as an alternative to the double-decker, and a particularly attractive alternative later in the decade as SBG became disenchanted with

▲ Western SMT was quick to see the benefits of 36ft-long coaches for its Glasgow to London service, and in 1963–64 put 16 Leopard PSU3s on to the route. These seated 38, which meant that the 16 Y-types had between them the same capacity as the 20 30ft-long Leopard 30-seaters introduced to the London run in 1960. So four fewer vehicles (and their crews) could carry the same number of passengers. They were attractive buses in Western's black and white livery, and had illuminated fleetname panels. They also had a polished surround to the grille area, quadruple headlights and a chrome bumper. KL1826 (VCS 380) makes a refreshment stop at Lockerbie in September 1964. The service took 12 hours, with departures from both Glasgow and London at 8am and 8pm. There were 13 intermediate timing points in Scotland alone, including some which sounded spectacularly unimpressive for a trunk service, such as Lesmahagow (New Bridge) and Millbank (AA Box). South of the border the service was routed via Penrith, the A66 to Scotch Corner, and then by the A1 to London.

rear-engined Fleetlines and VRTs. A 36ft-long Y-type bus seated 53, the same number of seats as on the early postwar double-deckers which they were replacing for much of the 1960s. And, in theory at least, they could carry 24 standing passengers.

In the 1960s the Y-type was supplied to SBG on AEC Reliance, Leyland Tiger Cub, Leyland Leopard, Albion Viking, Bedford VAM, Bristol LH and Bristol RE chassis. By 1969 there were around 850 in SBG service, making up almost 25 per cent of the group's fleet, and that number would be more than doubled by the time the last Y-type was delivered to SBG in 1983, when new Y-types were replacing old Y-types.

Successful as the Y-type undoubtedly was, it was in the end a coach produced by a bus builder. Only two Scottish independents bought new Y-type coaches. The Scottish Co-operative Wholesale Society, which used the rather catchier Majestic name for part of its coach business, bought five Y-types on 36ft Reliance chassis. And two similar coaches were bought by Hutchison of Overtown.

There were no significant changes to the basic design in the 1960s, although there would be updates in the 1970s. ■

▲ Along with the London coaches Western took a small number of 49-seaters with short windows, and these were in the red and cream used for coaches on less prestigious work than express services or tours. DL1840 (VCS 394), a 1963 coach, pauses in Whitesands, Dumfries, on the Glasgow to Carlisle service. Later in the decade coaches of this type received red skirt panels. Note the simpler grille treatment compared with the coach in the previous picture.

▼ There were shorter Y-types too, with a nominal length of 31ft, initially built on Leyland Tiger Cub and AEC Reliance chassis. A 1964 Reliance of Scottish Omnibuses, Bathgate-based ZB98B (AFS 98B), is parked in Dunoon on a private hire. It was one of 13 short Reliances delivered to SOL in 1964 and had 41 seats. When new it was in the company's light green and cream livery; in 1966 it received the new dark green and the associated Eastern Scottish fleetname.

▼ Aberdeen Corporation chose the combination of Tiger Cub chassis and Y-type body for its first new one-man-operated buses. These were the only Y-types with two doors. Twelve were delivered in 1966–67, and the first, which reverted to fleet number 1 (ERG 1D) for single-deckers, is seen in Market Street when new. They were 43-seaters and were Aberdeen's first-ever new Leylands. They were also Scotland's last new Tiger Cubs.

▼ The five Y-type coaches supplied to Central SMT on Albion Viking chassis in 1966 were unusual in not having roof-mounted destination displays. They also had a single-piece inswing door, rather than the standard air-operated jacknife doors. The red piping insert in the polished metal trim was an attractive detail on these unusual coaches which were only operated by Central for 12 months. In 1967 they were transferred to Highland Omnibuses, having been replaced by new Duple-bodied Bedford VAMs, which is what Central had wanted in the first place. This is AC4 (FGM 104D).

Dundee and its hinterland

I don't want to besmirch the good name of Dundee, but for bus enthusiasts in the Scottish central belt in the 1960s the city famed for jam, jute and journalism didn't have the appeal of the country's other big cities. Glasgow and Edinburgh were more easily accessible. Aberdeen was further, but it was by any standards nicer, and a holiday resort to boot. It even had a sandy beach, which was fine if you were looking out to sea because it was a bit industrial on the landward side. Industrial Dundee seemed just a shade drab, an impression boosted by the dull green livery of its municipal buses as they travelled through canyons of grey tenements.

▲ Dundee Corporation's livery had been simplified during the 1950s, with the final version featuring white window surrounds and a line or two of orange relief. A few buses were running in this livery in the early part of the 1960s, including 11 (BTS 491), one of ten 1951 Brush-bodied Daimler CVD6s which were the operator's last half-cab single-deckers. They were 30ft-long 39-seaters and were withdrawn in 1968.

The presence of independents – McLennan of Spittalfield, Greyhound of Arbroath – seemed little recompense, although from 1962 the yellow of Alexander Northern injected some colour. Dundee was a city where, from 1966, you could regularly see buses of all three Alexander companies. Northern operated locally from a depot adjacent to the bus station in the city centre. Midland ran services from Perth, Stirling and Glasgow. And with the opening of the Tay Road Bridge Fife's red buses added extra colour.

The Dundee Corporation fleet was slightly bigger than that of Aberdeen, and just as varied. All 19 of its wartime Daimlers were still in operation in 1960, heavily rebuilt, and they would survive until 1965. Early postwar purchases were a mix of AECs and Daimlers with a variety of bodies – Alexander, Barnard, Brockhouse, Brush, Croft, Metro-Cammell, Northern Coachbuilders and Weymann. These included some rear-entrance half-cab single-deckers which entered service as late as 1951. To speed tram replacement Dundee bought ex-London buses. Ten STL-class AEC Regents, new in 1946, were purchased in 1955 and operated until 1964. They were followed in 1956 by 30 seven-year-old Cravens-bodied RTs, which ran until

▲ There was no lack of variety in the Dundee fleet in the 1960s. Among the older buses which would run until the end of the decade were three 1950 AEC Regent IIIs with Clydebank-built Brockhouse bodies, including 147 (BTS 117). These had been rebuilt with rubber-mounted windows. Bodies of this style were bought by all four Scottish municipal fleets. The unusual car on the left is a 1964 rear-engined Renault 1100.

▼ A contrast in Dundonian Daimlers at the Corporation's Dock Street terminus. Nearest the camera is 131 (BTS 471), a 1951 CVD6, one of ten bodied by Croft of Glasgow. On the right is 1949 bus 116 (ATS 906) which originally had a Barnard body. There had been ten of these Barnard-bodied CVD6s, all of which were rebodied by Alexander in 1959–60 with an unusual five-bay version of the builder's standard four-bay body. Contemporaneous rebodies of Daimlers for Aberdeen used the standard body, as shown on page 61. As with many of the vehicles illustrated in this volume these two buses are advertising liquid refreshment, with the choice of milk or whisky. The Croft-bodied buses operated for around 20 years; the Alexander rebodies for around 23.

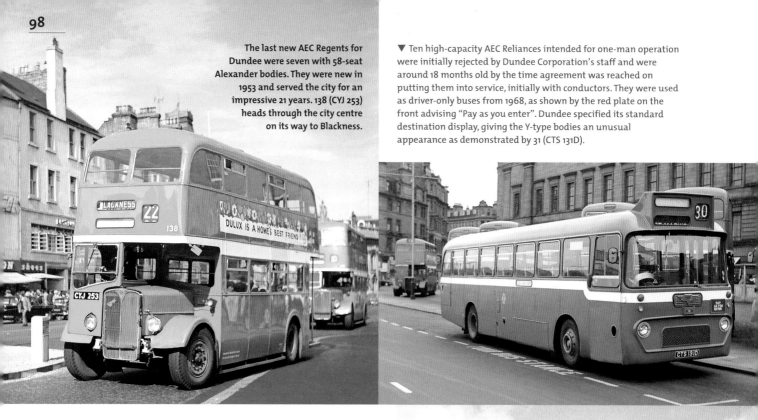

The last new AEC Regents for Dundee were seven with 58-seat Alexander bodies. They were new in 1953 and served the city for an impressive 21 years. 138 (CYJ 253) heads through the city centre on its way to Blackness.

▼ Ten high-capacity AEC Reliances intended for one-man operation were initially rejected by Dundee Corporation's staff and were around 18 months old by the time agreement was reached on putting them into service, initially with conductors. They were used as driver-only buses from 1968, as shown by the red plate on the front advising "Pay as you enter". Dundee specified its standard destination display, giving the Y-type bodies an unusual appearance as demonstrated by 31 (CTS 131D).

1968–69. New buses in the mid 1950s were mainly Daimler CVG6s with Metro-Cammell Orion bodies of which there were 75. They were delivered between 1955 and 1958 and made up almost one-third of the fleet.

The last CVG6s, seven with Alexander bodies, were delivered in 1960 and the next new buses did not arrive until 1964, with 20 Alexander-bodied Fleetlines – stylish new buses, same drab old livery. By 1969 there were 65 Fleetlines in operation. Ten AEC Reliances with Alexander Y-type 53-seat bodies intended for one-man-operation were ordered in 1961, but were not built until 1964 and were not delivered until 1965 when they met with resistance from the trade union. So they promptly headed back to the coachbuilder's factory in Falkirk where they were stored prior to being re-delivered in 1966 when they finally entered service, initially crew-operated. But they paved the way for one-man-operated Swifts at the end of the decade. Dundee Corporation had three depots, Lochee Road, Marchbanks and Maryfield. In 1969 the Corporation was planning to sell its bus operation to the Scottish Bus Group but, as with a similar plan in Glasgow, this did not happen.

Arbroath lies 20 miles north-east of Dundee and was the base of Greyhound Coaches, which in 1961 took over the operations of Hunter & Nelson and ran a number of local services. And 20 miles to the northwest was Spittalfield, the headquarters of McLennan which ran a network of routes embracing Perth, Errol, Stanley, Blairgowrie and Dundee. ■

▲ The Alexander-bodied Fleetline 78-seater was the standard Dundee double-decker from 1964. On these even the cream band above the lower deck windows was abandoned, the only relief being the cream advert panels. 38 (CYJ 838D) is a 1966 bus which, like all double-deckers at that time, was crew-operated. By 1969 there were 65 Fleetlines in service.

▶ Alexander Northern provided a welcome splash of colour in Dundee. In 1962 Northern tried a variety of layouts for its new yellow livery. RB194 (KWG 655), seen in Dundee bus station in the summer of 1962, was an early repaint with a cream roof and upper deck window surrounds. There were just nine double-deckers, all Leyland Titans, at Northern's Dundee depot in the 1960s.

◀ Alexander Northern NA34 (AWG 621) is a 1947 Alexander-bodied AEC Regal on the service to Inchture, which lies between Dundee and Perth. The conductress keeps a watchful eye from the entrance steps. At the start of the 1960s Northern operated 78 Regals which made up almost 20 per cent of the fleet.

The last AEC Regals for Alexander were six which entered service in the summer of 1951. The chassis were ordered by Sutherland of Peterhead, whose business had been taken over by Alexander in March 1950. Northern's NA99 (DMS 125) heads for Auchterhouse. It has a 35-seat Alexander body.

▲ Greyhound had operations in Sheffield as well as in Scotland, and 108 (GRH 193) carries "Greyhound Sheffield" lettering on the front. It is a 1944 Guy Arab II with postwar Roe bodywork, and it had been new to East Yorkshire Motor Services who specified the unusual roof profile which allowed its buses to pass through the arch of the North Bar in Beverley. It is seen in Arbroath, on the Friockheim service.

▲ It was extremely unusual for Scottish Bus Group vehicles to be sold for further service with independent operators. Greyhound had a number of these ex-Scottish Omnibuses 1953 AEC Regal IVs with 38-seat Alexander bodies, including KSC 550 which is seen in Arbroath in 1967.

McLennan operated services from Perth north to Stanley and Spittalfield, and east to Errol. This unusual vehicle, DGS 625, is a 30ft-long Leyland Tiger PS1/3, one of a pair with 39-seat McLennan bodies which entered service in 1951. Both survive in preservation.

▼ Blairgowrie in Perthshire was served by three operators in the mid-1960s, Northern, which had a depot in the town, McLennan of Spittalfield and McLachlan of Bridge of Cally. The bus on the left is one of many rebuilds in the McLennan fleet. It had started life in 1939 as a Leyland Titan TD7c double-decker with Birmingham Corporation. It was acquired by McLennan in 1950 and operated until 1953. The chassis was then lengthened to 30ft and fitted with a new 39-seat McLennan-built body, re-entering service in 1955 with new Perthshire registration GGS 688 in place of its original Birmingham mark, FOF 281. In its new incarnation it operated until 1968. The unusual little bus next to it, NES 231, is a 1960 Thames Trader 611E light truck chassis with 24-seat Strachans body, bought new by McLachlan. The McLachlan business was taken over by McLennan in 1967.

Harrington

In the days before motorways, Hove, the location of coachbuilder Harrington, was a long way from Scotland. Which in part explains the rarity of the company's products in the country. Just 11 new Harrington-bodied coaches were supplied to Scottish operators in the 1960s, with the last being delivered to BOAC at Prestwick in 1964. These were two 36ft AEC Reliances and followed an earlier BOAC Prestwick Harrington Crusader on an unusual petrol-engined Thames Trader 568E chassis; the standard Thames coach was the diesel-powered 570E.

Harrington's most northerly customer, McIntyre of Bucksburn, was around 600 miles from Hove – quite a delivery run for the new AEC Reliances which the company bought. McIntyre, incidentally, aimed at giving its holiday tour customers greater comfort by specifying 37 rather than the normal 41 seats in its 30ft-long coaches. ∎

▲ Two 36ft AEC Reliances with Harrington Grenadier 51-seat bodies were delivered to the British Overseas Airways Corporation in 1964 for operation between its Glasgow terminal and Prestwick Airport. BOAC's O419F (AAG 650B) is seen in St Enoch Square, Glasgow. An unusual but decidedly 1960s feature is the use of groups of differently coloured headrest covers on the seats, red and grey. The quaint little red sandstone building in the background is St Enoch station on the Glasgow Underground. It survives today as a coffee shop.

1960s Harrington deliveries to Scottish operators		
BOAC, Prestwick	Thames 568E	1
BOAC, Prestwick	AEC Reliance	2
Comfort, Dunfermline	Bedford SB5	1
Garelochhead Coach Services	Thames 570E	3
Irvine, Salsburgh	Thames 570E	1
McConnachie, Eaglesham	Thames 570E	1
McIntyre, Bucksburn	AEC Reliance	2

The Kingdom of Fife

Local bus operation in Fife was dominated by Alexander or, from 1961, the new Alexander Fife company. There were independents in the region, generally small, and most of them running coaches or providing contract services for coal miners. The main exception was Niven of St Andrews, running a local route in the university town until selling out to Fife in 1967. The Alexander Fife fleet numbered 516 buses at its formation in 1961, and in 1962 a new Ayres red livery was adopted which quickly replaced Alexander's blue.

Most of the buses operated by Alexander Fife were Guys, Leylands and Bristols. From 1962 the company started buying AEC

▲ Guy Arab IIs with Northern Counties bodies were part of the Fife bus scene until 1968, by which time the oldest had 24 years of service behind them. FRO517 (AMS 232) is seen in Kirkcaldy bus station with Town Service lettering on the front and in the window over the rear wheel. This was introduced in 1962 when Fife adopted Ayres red as its livery – under the previous Alexander regime town service buses in Kirkcaldy had been dark red while the rest of the fleet was blue.

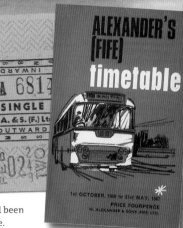

ALEXANDER'S
(FIFE)
timetable

1st OCTOBER, 1960 to 31st MAY, 1961

PRICE FOURPENCE

W. ALEXANDER & SONS (FIFE) LTD.

▶ The Leyland Tiger PS1 was the most numerous type in Alexander's early postwar orders, and when the company was divided in 1961 Tigers were to be found operating for all three of the new businesses. A 1947 Fife bus, FPA23 (AWG 558), is seen in Dunfermline depot, alongside a 1954 Wolseley 4/44. Fife had 45 PS1s, all of which were withdrawn by 1969.

▶ SMT's first postwar double-deckers were 40 AEC Regent IIIs which entered service in 1948 and had austere-looking 53-seat Alexander lowbridge bodies which were little different in appearance from the bodies the company built during the war. BB60A (FFS 181) is in Kirkcaldy in 1965 carrying the short-lived Scottish fleetname. Most of these Regents were operated until 1968–69, latterly in dark Lothian green. It was unusual to find such an elderly bus on the services running across the Forth Road Bridge from Edinburgh.

▼ All 20 Guy Arab LUFs in the Alexander fleet were in the Fife area, and all had this style of Alexander 41-seat coach body. At different times they carried coach and then bus livery. The last, FGA20 (JWG 511), was new in 1957 and is seen leaving Dunfermline for Oakley.

◄ The biggest batch of highbridge buses bought by Alexander after the war comprised 25 Guy Arab IIIs with 56-seat Cravens bodies, delivered in 1948. All were in the Fife area, and were operated until 1969–70. FRO589 (AWG 375) pauses in Cowdenbeath on the frequent service from Ballingry to Dunfermline. A vehicle from this batch was among the first Scottish buses to be preserved.

Reliances, building up a fleet of 59 by 1966. Albion Vikings dominated single-deck orders from 1965, and one batch of Bristol RELLs was delivered in 1968. New double-deckers in the 1960s were Bristol Lodekkas until 1967, and Daimler Fleetlines from 1968. The company also operated 39 Lowlanders at the end of the decade, seven delivered new in 1963, and the remainder transferred from Central SMT and Western SMT between 1965 and 1967.

The make-up of the fleet changed dramatically during the 1960s. There were 197 Guys in operation in 1961; but just over 30 in 1969. The number of Bristols climbed in the same period from 100 to 177. Alexander Fife had ten depots with almost half of the fleet, around 250 buses, being allocated to its two biggest at Dunfermline and Kirkcaldy. ■

Odd buses were always an attraction for enthusiasts, and in Fife these included two 1950 Titans with highbridge Leyland bodywork which had been Leyland stock vehicles. FRB102 (CWG 296) pulls out of Dunfermline bus station on the service to High Valleyfield, with advertising for the company's parcel service. A Bristol Lodekka FS6G on the Leven service loads in the adjacent platform.

▶ A busy scene at Dunfermline bus station in 1965. Nearest the camera is a 1952 Leyland Royal Tiger PSU1/15 with Alexander body, FPC53 (DWG 772). It was one of six similar coaches in the Fife fleet, three of which were rebuilt in the mid 1960s with front entrances to make them more suitable for bus operation. The other vehicles are, from the left, a 1964 AEC Reliance with Alexander Y-type bus body, and two Midland buses, a 1956 Tiger Cub and a 1965 Leopard. The town's 1934 art deco fire station is in the background. The building is being developed as an arts centre.

▼ The oldest vehicles acquired by the Alexander Fife company on its formation in 1961 included Leyland Tigers dating back to 1937. P609 (WG 9002) was a 1940 TS8 with 39-seat Alexander body which was withdrawn in 1963 and is seen here leaving Kirkcaldy depot pursued by an Esso Bedford.

▲ ▶ Before the opening of Perth bus station in 1966, the forecourt of the railway station was one of the starting points for out-of-town services. These photographs show two of the liveries applied to Fife's dual-purpose Tiger Cubs, and detail differences in the Alexander body of the late 1950s. FPD111 (KMS 480) was new in 1958 and is in bus livery, which would later be improved by painting the area around the windows cream. FPD195 (OMS 271) dated from 1960 and is in Fife's original coach livery; this was later revised with a cream roof, as seen on the Guy illustrated on page 103. In a game of spot the difference on the Tiger Cubs, key changes on the later body are the grille, the replacement of the full-width bumper by moulding strips, the absence of the little V-shaped dip in the centre of the moulding below the windscreen, and different treatment of the skirt panels within the wheelbase. And that's not mentioning the seats, lights, indicators, and driver's windscreen.

▶ The first Bedfords for Fife were four VAS1s in 1962, three coaches and a bus. A fourth coach, FW5 (BXA 608B), was added in 1964, and is seen here on a tour to Aberdeen. The Duple Bella Vista was a neat little coach and was bought in the early 1960s by SBG companies Fife, Midland, Northern and Scottish Omnibuses, and also by MacBrayne. All of Fife's Bedfords were withdrawn in 1972.

◄ The Bedford OB with Duple Vista body was a classic coach of the 1940s, bought by operators large and small. Over 300 were bought new by Scottish companies, some with Vista bodies built in Edinburgh by SMT, and many were still in service at the start of the 1960s. The OB was powered by a 72bhp 3.5-litre petrol engine, and with 29-seat Vista body weighed just 3tons 14cwt unladen. BWG 39 had an SMT body and had been new to Alexander in 1948. It passed to Midland in 1961 and was bought by Low of Tomintoul the following year. It ran for Low until 1969.

Independent coaching

There was considerable variety in the fleets of small coach operators at the start of the 1960s, when many companies were still operating vehicles built in the late 1940s and early 1950s. Half-cab coaches were generally used only for school or contract work, as were older heavyweight underfloor-engined models – and, of course, it was these types which attracted most enthusiasts rather than the more common Bedfords and Thames Traders. It's also worth noting that the speed limit for coaches at the start of the 1960s was just 30mph. It was raised to 40mph in 1961, and to 50mph in 1966.

By the end of the decade, very few pre-1960 coaches were to be found on front-line work, as independent operators in growing numbers invested in the new lightweight VAL and VAM models from Bedford, and the Ford R-series and, to a lesser extent, the heavier-duty models from AEC and Leyland. ∎

▶ The bonneted Leyland Comet CPO1 was never a common model in the UK, and the number in use in Scotland in the 1960s was in single figures. Plaxton-bodied AYJ 867 was operated by McLeod of Helmsdale. It had been new in 1949 to Dickson of Dundee. The Comet was powered by a vertical Leyland 5.08-litre O.300 engine, a precursor of the O.350 more familiar to bus engineers in its horizontal form in the Tiger Cub.

▶ Full-width cabs were specified by a few operators of front-engined coaches, including Young's of Paisley, the original owner of this 1949 Maudslay Marathon III with 33-seat Brockhouse body. It was operated by Western SMT from 1951 to 1960, and then by Mitchell of Luthermuir from 1960 to 1966. It is seen outside Mitchell's garage. The Mitchell business was purchased by Northern in 1967 following the death of the proprietor.

▼ The Burlingham Seagull was widely regarded as a 1950s classic, and many of these impressive coaches were still in operation in the 1960s. This Leyland Royal Tiger was, in 1951, the first underfloor-engined coach in the fleet of West Coast Motor Services of Campbeltown, and is seen in the company's depot in the mid 1960s. SB 8500 would be modelled by Corgi Classics 30 years later.

▶ The popularity of the Commer Avenger steadily declined through the 1950s, and by the 1960s annual sales to Scottish operators could be counted on the fingers of one hand. Anderson of Bonchester Bridge bought this Duple-bodied coach, KKS 112, in 1959. When fitted to a Commer this style of body – most familiar on Bedford chassis as the Super Vega – was known as the Corinthian. The last new Scottish Avenger was bought by King of Dunblane in 1962. Commer was part of the Rootes group, which would re-use the Avenger name for a Hillman car in 1970.

Ford made considerable inroads into Bedford's coach business in the 1960s, initially with the Thames Trader 570E, a direct competitor for the Bedford SB. This was followed in 1963 by the bigger 676E, marketed as the Thames 36, and then by the new R-series, introduced in 1965, at which point the Thames name was dropped in favour of Ford. FVA 679D was one of two R192s with Plaxton 45-seat bodies bought by Whiteford of Lanark in 1966. It is seen in Lanark bus station.

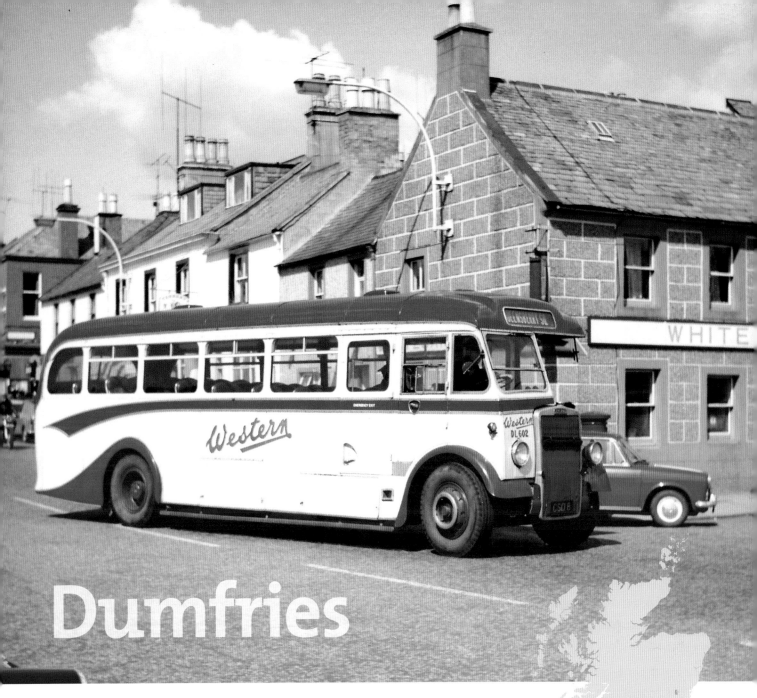

Dumfries

There was a small pocket of independent bus operation around Dumfries, a town where Western SMT was the major operator. Western had taken over the Caledonian Omnibus Co in 1950, a substantial business with 138 buses. By the mid 1960s Western had almost 150 buses allocated to Dumfries, a figure which included vehicles based at a number of outstations across the south-west of Scotland from Stranraer in the west to Lockerbie in the east. The main independents serving the town were Clark's of Glencaple, which was taken over by Western in 1965, Gibson's of Moffat, and Carruthers of New Abbey. All out-of-town services operated by Western and by the independents terminated at a bus stand on Whitesands, alongside the River Nith. ∎

▲ The last half-cab single-deckers ordered by Western SMT were 16 Leyland Tiger PS1s with Alexander 35-seat coach bodies. They operated from 1949 to 1965. Western's cream and red coach livery encapsulated the best of old-fashioned coaching with the red side flash sweeping down at the rear, and with Western's script fleetname. While other SBG companies repainted half-cab coaches like this in bus livery as they aged, Western's PS1s carried this paint scheme for their entire lives. Although Western bought Leyland double-deckers through the 1950s, after the PS1s its next single-deckers from Leyland would not be delivered until 1960. DL602 (CSD 8) looks well in this 1965 view.

▲ This style of Alexander body was usually fitted out as a 41-seat coach, but Western SMT specified it for a batch of 16 superior 44-seat buses – note the high-backed seats – delivered on Guy Arab LUF chassis in 1955. They were operated until 1968. This style of body usually had an emergency door in the short centre bay but the Western buses had the emergency exit on the rear. This maximised seating capacity, which would have been reduced had space been provided between the seats alongside the short bay to meet legal requirements on access to a side-mounted emergency exit. This is KG1116 (GCS 201) from Kilmarnock depot.

▼ Clark's only operated two vehicles when it was taken over by Western in 1965. FJA 612 was a 1953 Leyland-bodied Royal Tiger, purchased from the North Western Road Car Co in 1962. It was immediately sold by Western. Here it heads for Glencaple, where Clark's was based.

▲ At first glance looking like any other Western Lodekka, this 1961 bus was one of a pair of 30ft-long FL6G models with 70 seats, ten more than the standard LD6G. These were the only rear-entrance 30ft Lodekkas supplied to SBG, and both were initially based in Dumfries. From 1962 Western would standardise on the forward-entrance FLF6G. DB1624 (RAG 390) heads to Lincluden on a Dumfries local service in 1965.

◄ Gibson's Leyland Tiger Cub LVD 263 waits at Whitesands, ready to return to Moffat. Although looking like a typical 1950s SBG purchase, this Alexander-bodied vehicle had been new to Hutchison of Overtown in 1955. It was part of a stock build order placed by Leyland dealer Millburn Motors. Originally a 41-seat coach, it was bought by Gibson's in 1957 and re-fitted with 45 bus seats, presumably overcoming whatever problem Western had with certification for the emergency exit layout when specifying its Guy buses in 1955. Gibson's sold it in 1967 to Mitchell of Luthermuir and it did eventually join SBG when Mitchell was purchased by Northern later that year.

Western service 5 operated from Glasgow to Carlisle via Kilmarnock, Cumnock, Sanquhar, Dumfries and Annan. Few if any passengers would travel the entire length of the 5 hour 50 minute route, but there would still be many making long interurban trips, justifying the use of a modern bus like 1967 Daimler Fleetline CR2174 (JAG 527F) from Cumnock depot, seen crossing the River Nith at Auldgirth on a bridge long since closed to traffic and bypassed by a new road alignment.

Albion: Sure as the sunrise

At the start of the 1960s there were quite a few Glasgow-built Albion coaches in regular use around Scotland. The oldest were front-engined Valkyries dating back to the late 1940s. Then came small numbers of Valiants, and rather larger numbers of the lightweight Victor. Four mid-engined Aberdonians were supplied new to Scottish independents, and there were 26 running for SBG – 23 at Alexander and three at Western SMT. All of these dated from 1957–58.

The smaller Nimbus was around in smaller numbers, two supplied new to independents and, by the end of 1960, 21 in SBG service – 15 at Alexander and Lawson, and six with Highland. A few Nimbuses and Aberdonians which had been supplied new to English operators migrated north in the 1960s.

The Albion-engined FT39 Victor was phased out in the late 1950s, but a new model, the Leyland-engined VT21L, was introduced in 1962. This was designed as an alternative to the Bedford SB and Thames 570E. It met with some success south of the border, but just 13 were bought new by Scottish operators, including four for Hutchison of Overtown, the biggest user. They entered service between 1963 and 1966, and all had Duple's attractive Firefly body, built in the former Burlingham factory in Blackpool.

Then came the Viking, and suddenly Albion was once again a power in Scottish coaching, as the three Alexander companies from 1965 embraced the new rear-engined VK43 as the successor to the Leyland Tiger Cub and the short AEC Reliance. By the end of 1969 there were 223 in SBG service. The final total, in 1970, would be 228, including a solitary VK49 with Pneumocyclic gearbox. One VK43, with rare Park Royal coach bodywork, was bought by Clyde Coast. ∎

The Albion Victor of the late 1940s was available with either a petrol engine, in the FT3AB, or a diesel, in the FT39N. Most of those operated in Scotland were bodied by Scottish Aviation or by Duple, as with OUP 934 in the fleet of Lennox of Whiting Bay. The Victor was normally a 31-seater.

▶ The Nimbus was what would be known to later generations as a midibus, and while it seemed like the ideal vehicle for rural routes, it found relatively few buyers in Scotland. Highland Omnibuses bought six in 1956. A3 (KST 52) is seen outside Thurso depot. The 29-seat body was by Alexander. All were withdrawn by 1967 – an 11-year life compared with 16 years for Highland's contemporary Reliances.

▶ After the 1961 Alexander split, Northern became the biggest Scottish operator of the Aberdonian, with 17 which it inherited from Alexander plus three acquired from Western SMT, where they were non-standard. NNL23 (RSC 427), seen in Glasgow in 1965, was an oddity in that it briefly carried the large bus-style fleetname, uniquely on this type of body, while its Edinburgh registration identifies it as the coach which was at the 1957 Scottish Motor Show and then ran for Scottish Omnibuses for six months in 1958 before being transferred to Alexander.

▶ The last new Nimbuses in Scotland were ten 29-seat coaches supplied to Alexander and Lawson in 1960 for tours in the Highlands, where there were still many single-track roads unsuitable for bigger coaches. All ten passed to Midland in 1961. They had stylish Alexander bodies which made full use of the evolving glass fibre technology to create interesting shapes for the front and rear. These neat vehicles weighed just 4 tons 3 cwt 2 qrs unladen and were powered by Albion's 4.1-litre 72bhp EN250 engine. With its Alexander's fleetname, only the legal lettering shows that N12 (OMS 245) was in Midland ownership when photographed in Glasgow in 1963.

▼ The VT21L version of the Victor was introduced in 1962, and most had Duple (Northern) Firefly bodies, as seen on this Lancashire-registered Albion demonstrator, CTB 739B, at Crieff Golf Course in 1965. The legal lettering records Leyland Motors as the owner.

The front-engined Viking VK41L was primarily an export chassis, but one was bodied by Alexander as a 41-seat bus for operation in Britain. It was an exhibit at the 1963 Scottish Motor Show in Glasgow's Kelvin Hall and was then tried by Midland for six months in the winter of 1964–65, operating from Perth depot as MN16 (BWG 650B). Here it loads outside the Midland office in Tay Street, on the service to Dundee. In the summer of 1965 it was sold by Albion to Barrie of Balloch and by 1968 it was running for Lochs of Crossbost on the island of Lewis, where it ended its days.

◀ This Scottish Omnibuses AEC Reliance, B910A (YWS 910), was the first 36ft-long coach to enter service in Scotland, in April 1962. This is a 1965 view, after it had been repainted in Lothian green. The combination of a cream roof and green skirt was unusual; Y-type coaches generally only had green window surrounds. It is loading in Edinburgh for the overnight service to London.

The move to longer buses

The use of 36ft-long buses was legalised in July 1961. The first for Scottish operators were at the 1961 Scottish Motor Show in November, a three-door Leyland Leopard for Edinburgh Corporation and a toilet-equipped AEC Reliance coach for Scottish Omnibuses. These had the first Alexander Y-type bodies and both entered service in 1962.

The first 36ft coach for an independent also entered service in 1962, an AEC Reliance with Duple Continental 51-seat body for Dodds of Troon. Acceptance of 36ft-long coaches was slow, in part because the vast majority of family-run coach businesses were buying lower-cost lightweight Thames and Bedford models. The arrival of the Bedford VAL boosted sales of 36ft coaches from 1963, but they still remained a minority interest for small operators throughout the decade, most of whom were happy to standardise on 45-seaters based on the 32ft-long Bedford VAM and Ford R192 which were introduced in 1965

The first 36ft-long service buses for independents were two Plaxton-bodied Reliances for Irvine of Salsburgh and a Northern Counties-bodied Leopard for AA member Young of Ayr, all delivered in 1963. MacBrayne took small numbers of 36ft buses from 1964.

The Scottish Bus Group embraced longer single-deckers with enthusiasm from 1963, building up large fleets of both buses and coaches with Y-type bodies. By 1969 there were some 530 36ft-long vehicles in SBG service. ∎

The move to 36ft-long single-deckers started slowly, but gathered pace as the 1960s progressed. The first for MacBrayne were two AEC Reliances in 1964. These had 53-seat Willowbrook bodies and were the company's biggest buses. They were used on local services in Fort William and were initially crew-operated. The glazed cove panels were an unusual feature on vehicles intended primarily for local bus operation, and made for a bright interior.

Lanarkshire

The main operator in Lanarkshire was Central SMT which had depots at Carluke, East Kilbride, Hamilton, Motherwell and Wishaw, housing between them 500 vehicles. But other SBG companies served the county too. Scottish Omnibuses operated in the adjoining towns of Airdrie and Coatbridge and had a depot in Airdrie, while Alexander operated to Airdrie from Falkirk, and Western SMT ran to Airdrie from Kilmarnock.

There were four substantial independents in Lanarkshire, three of which would sell their businesses to SBG. The first to sell was Chieftain of Hamilton, which operated 31 buses in and around Hamilton and East Kilbride. The business was bought by Central SMT

▲ Chieftain of Hamilton operated 31 vehicles, most of them double-deck buses. These included 16 ex-London Transport RTL-class Leyland Titans. 53 (JXN 333), new in 1948 as LT's RTL13, is seen in Churchill Avenue in the centre of East Kilbride in the spring of 1961 heading for Hairmyres. In the background there is a 1954 Ford Popular. Central acquired the Chieftain business in October 1961.

in October 1961. The fleet included a large number of ex-London Transport RTL-class Leyland Titans, and two Leyland Atlanteans. The takeover established Central's position as the sole local bus operator in the expanding East Kilbride new town.

Coatbridge and Airdrie formed the hub of Baxter's operations, which were purchased by Scottish Omnibuses at the end of 1962. The two towns were at the heart of Scotland's heavy engineering, and Baxter's ran an intensive service network, operated in the main by lowbridge Leyland double-deckers. The network of rail lines which connected industrial sites in the area meant there were many low bridges to contend with. Despite serving an area in which heavy industry dominated, the 53 vehicles in Baxter's fleet were always smartly turned-out. It was also the youngest fleet of any significant Scottish bus operator with an average age of just 4.5 years reflecting the company's regular investment in new vehicles.

An intriguing might-have-been was an application by Baxter's to the Scottish Traffic Commissioner in 1961 for permission to run 36ft-long single-deckers on all its routes, giving it an alternative to

▲ There were 22 Titans in the Baxter's fleet, all of them exposed-radiator PD2s. The oldest had Leyland bodies including two PD2/10s delivered in 1953. They were operated until 1968. This is Coatbridge town centre, an area which would change beyond recognition in the 1970s, with 55 (HVD 60) heading to Lomond Road. The destination display offered detailed route information at the expense of legibility.

Most of Baxter's single-deckers were AECs, but there were a few Leylands as illustrated by Royal Tiger 101 (HVA 883) which had been new in 1952 and had a 44-seat Leyland body. The fleet number started a new series for single-deck service buses which had reached 121 when the Baxter's business was bought by SOL. The location is Graham Street, Airdrie.

◄ The oldest double-deckers in the Baxter's fleet at the time of the SOL takeover were two 1950 Leyland-bodied Titans which were among the company's few second-hand buses. They had been new to Irvine of Salsburgh. SOL started repainting the fleet green and these two vehicles, HH29/30V (FVD 224/5), are in slightly different liveries; the bus in the background has an additional band of cream relief below the upper deck windows.

▲ ▶ Scottish Omnibuses transferred four relatively new Bristol Lodekkas to the Baxter's fleet in 1963 and these initially operated in green with a B in the route number display to indicate a Baxter's service, as seen on AA892 (YWS 892) passing Airdrie bus station. However in 1964 they were among the first buses to be repainted blue, as shown by sister vehicle AA893V (YWS 893) in Coatbridge, fresh out of the paint shop and also carrying a Baxter's fleet number, 93. AA892 has an advert exhorting: "Don't ask a man to drink and drive", gender-specific language which seems old-fashioned half a century later.

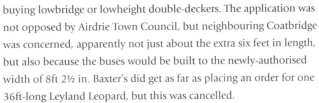

buying lowbridge or lowheight double-deckers. The application was not opposed by Airdrie Town Council, but neighbouring Coatbridge was concerned, apparently not just about the extra six feet in length, but also because the buses would be built to the newly-authorised width of 8ft 2½ in. Baxter's did get as far as placing an order for one 36ft-long Leyland Leopard, but this was cancelled.

The Baxter's takeover by SOL was to evolve in unexpected ways. In 1963 a start was made on repainting the fleet. Around half of Baxter's buses had been repainted green when there was an about-turn in 1964. Most of the green buses were then repainted back in to Baxter's blue. Also repainted blue were four 1962 FLF Lodekkas which SOL had transferred to the Baxter's fleet immediately after the takeover.

Carmichael's Highland Bus Service, based in Glenboig, ran from Coatbridge to Moodiesburn and Kilsyth, and operated a town service in Cumbernauld, in neighbouring Dunbartonshire. It ran 30 vehicles. The frequency of the Moodiesburn service was increased in 1960 to run half-hourly throughout the day, part of the justification being a lack of pubs in the village. Reporting on the licence hearing before the Scottish Traffic Commissioner, *Commercial Motor*

▲ At the time of the SOL takeover Baxter's had on order one Daimler Fleetline. It was delivered to SOL in October 1963, and was one of the first lowheight examples of Alexander's new body for rear-engined chassis, technically the D-type although seldom referred to as such. It was also SBG's first new rear-engined bus. DD961A (9961 SF) initially ran in green from New Street depot in Edinburgh, as seen here in Bathgate on the service from Glasgow to Edinburgh. However within 12 months it was transferred to the Baxter's fleet, repainted in Baxter's livery and given a Baxter fleet number, 79, following on from the company's last AEC Bridgemaster. It was until 1965 the only Fleetline in SBG service. It would be rebodied by Alexander in 1966 after its original body was destroyed by fire.

magazine noted: "One witness said that there were 60 public houses in Coatbridge but not one place of refreshment in Moodiesburn." Which nicely sums up 1960s Coatbridge.

The Carmichael fleet was noteworthy for its collection of ageing Albions which were used mainly on services for coal miners. In the 1960s the company bought six new Leyland Leopards for the Coatbridge services, and a forward-entrance Leyland Titan for operation in Cumbernauld. The Carmichael business was taken over by Alexander Midland in August 1966. It continued to operate from Carmichael's Greenfoot garage until the start of 1968 when the operations were transferred to a new purpose-built depot in Cumbernauld, some five miles north.

The fourth of the big independents was Hutchison of Overtown. Double-deckers, Leyland Titans bought new, were part of the fleet until 1965, but for most of the 1960s the company's services, centred on Wishaw, were operated by smart AEC Reliances with Willowbrook bus bodies. Hutchison bought new coaches every year, generally running them for two or three years before selling them. And the company was a major supporter of AEC, buying 32 Reliances and four Swifts between 1960 and 1969, as well as buying

HIGHLAND BUS SERVICE

TIME TABLE

— 1966 —

COATBRIDGE TO KILSYTH
COATBRIDGE TO MOODIESBURN
KILSYTH TO CUMBERNAULD NEW TOWN
CUMBERNAULD NEW TOWN LOCAL

HIGHLAND BUS SERVICE
(Proprietor—JOHN CARMICHAEL)
GREENFOOT GARAGE (By Coatbridge)
Telephone—Office :   *Telephone—Garage :*
GLENBOIG 247   GLENBOIG 307

LUXURY COACHES
for
PRIVATE HIRE

▲ Four Willowbrook-bodied Leopard buses were purchased by Carmichael in 1963–64 and were usually to be found on the service from Coatbridge to Kilsyth, as illustrated by 687 FVD. They followed two Alexander-bodied Leopards purchased in 1961 which had been the company's first new service buses since an Albion Valiant in 1951. The Willowbrook Leopards would run with Midland until 1975.

▼ All of Carmichael's underfloor-engined buses carried a coach-like livery, as seen by ex-Glasgow Leyland Worldmaster LW2 (FYS 690). The Worldmasters were the only Carmichael buses to carry fleet numbers. Alongside at the company's Greenfoot depot is an ex-Ribble PD2, CCK346. The panel between the headlights of the Worldmaster is tartan. Both these buses were in operation when Midland took over in 1966.

◀ This Albion Valkyrie, DVD 905, was one of a pair purchased by Carmichael in 1948. For most of its life it ran in cream coach livery, but was repainted in red bus livery in 1964. It is in Glasgow's George Square where it is about to depart on a tour organised by the Scottish Branch of the Omnibus Society.

▶ Carmichael's Coatbridge terminus was little more than a piece of waste ground, as can be gathered by this view of Midland's ex-Carmichael Worldmaster MPF4 (FYS 687). It still displays the Highland name in what had been the route number box, and carries an Albion badge which had been fitted by Carmichael. Midland operated the Worldmasters until 1971.

▼ Double-deck operation by Hutchison of Overtown ended in 1965. This Leyland Titan PD2/30 with 59-seat lowbridge Northern Counties body, SVD 882, was one of the late survivors and had been the last double-decker bought by the company, in 1958. It is seen in Wishaw. It would see further service in Scotland with Cunningham's of Paisley.

For most of the 1960s Hutchison's services were operated mainly by Willowbrook-bodied AEC Reliances. This bus, 719 AVA, was new in 1961 and was a 30ft-long 45-seater. It is loading in Wishaw for Larkhall. Hutchison would later switch to 36ft-long 53-seaters.

lightweight coaches from Bedford, Ford and Albion. There were frequent confrontations before the Traffic Commissioner between Hutchison and Central SMT as the company sought licences to expand its route network.

The other independents were smaller. The best-known included Irvine of Salsburgh, which ran a service from Airdrie to Salsburgh and Shotts, generally with AEC Reliances. The company also operated a modern coach fleet under the Golden Eagle name. Further south another Irvine operated between Wishaw, Law (the company's base) and Carluke.

The town of Lanark was served by several small independents including McKnight, who ran a town service until selling out to Wilson of Carnwath in 1966. Stokes of Carstairs and Jackson of Auchenheath both operated services between Lanark and Lesmahagow. The Jackson service, with three buses, was taken over by Whiteford of Lanark in 1962. ∎

▲ The last rear-entrance single-deckers to enter service in Scotland were ten Guy Arab UFs for Central SMT, in 1954. This style of Alexander body was normally built as a centre-entrance coach, as illustrated on page 105, but it was Central's choice for this batch of 43-seat buses, and followed ten coaches delivered in 1952. K45 (GM 5945) is arriving in Lanark bus station. These unusual buses were withdrawn in 1966–67.

▲ This unusual Strachans-bodied Guy Arab IV was the regular vehicle on the service operated by Irvine of Law between Wishaw and Carluke. HVA 876 had been new in 1952 to the previous operator of the service, Duncan of Law, and was one of the first buses in Scotland with the Birmingham-style new-look front, used by both Guy and Daimler.

AEC Reliances which had been purchased new were the mainstay of the service operated by Irvine of Salsburgh between Airdrie and Shotts. Most had Willowbrook bodies, including WVA 454, one of a pair purchased in 1960. It is seen arriving at Airdrie bus station.

Vanishing independents

A number of small, and not so small, operators or their routes were taken over by other companies in the 1960s. The main takeovers were:

Year	Operator	Acquired by
1960	Greenshields, Salsburgh	Irvine, Salsburgh
1961	Bankfoot Motor Company	Alexander
	Chieftain, Hamilton	Central SMT
	Hunter & Nelson, Arbroath	T D Alexander (Greyhound)
1962	McDougall, Oban	Midland
	Baxter, Airdrie	Scottish Omnibuses
1963	Dickson, Dundee	Wallace Arnold
1964	Bain, North Erradale	Highland
	Ross, Balblair	Highland
	Mackenzie, Garve	Highland
	Mackintosh, Croy	Highland
	Smith, Newmains	Central SMT
	Stark's, Dunbar	Scottish Omnibuses
1965	Dunoon Motor Services	Cowal Motor Services
	Rothesay Motor Services	Western SMT
	Clark, Dumfries	Western SMT
	Achnasheen Hotel	Highland
	Fleming, Anstruther	Fife
	Strachan's, Ballater	Northern
	Newton, Dingwall	Highland
1966	Murray, Stranraer	Western SMT
	Carmichael, Glenboig	Midland
	Smith, Grantown-on-Spey	Highland
	Simpson's, Rosehearty	Northern
	Weir, Machrie	Bannatyne, Blackwaterfoot
	Ribbeck, Brodick	Lennox, Whiting Bay
	McKnight, Lanark	Wilson, Carnwath
1967	Lennox, Brodick	Arran Transport
	Lennox, Whiting Bay	Arran Transport
	Burnett's, Mintlaw	Northern
	MacGregor, Dornoch	Highland
	Burr, Tongue	Highland
	Robertson, Strathglass	Highland
	Niven, St Andrews	Fife
	Drysdale, Cupar	Fife
	Mitchell, Luthermuir	Northern
1968	Smith, Barrhead	Western SMT
	Kennedy, Kiltarlity	Highland
1969	McConnachie, Campbeltown	West Coast Motor Services

New vehicle deliveries to major operators 1960–1969

Operator	Approx Fleet size	1960	1961	1962	1963	1964	1965	1966	1967	1968	1969	Total	Yearly average intake	Yearly average required for 15-year life
SCOTTISH BUS GROUP														
Alexander	-	154	-	-	-	-	-	-	-	-	-	154	-	-
Alexander Fife	525	-	24	29	41	34	12	27	28	32	13	240	27	35
Alexander Midland	960	-	86	35	88	50	62	6	89	54	9	479	53	64
Alexander Northern	430	-	9	22	24	19	19	-	42	24	20	179	20	29
Central SMT	640	34	20	40	46	59	80	46	50	30	40	445	45	43
Highland Omnibuses	165	5	6	6	-	8	2	3	6	17	12	65	7	11
Scottish Omnibuses	880	60	60	72	54	67	38	106	20	45	24	546	55	59
Western SMT	1,050	75	80	42	137	71	107	59	62	26	49	708	71	70
SBG total	**4,650**	**328**	**285**	**246**	**390**	**308**	**320**	**247**	**297**	**228**	**167**	**2,816**	**282**	**310**
MUNICIPAL														
Aberdeen	225	12	10	8	11	8	8	18	16	12	15	118	12	15
Dundee	235	7	-	-	-	20	-	20	-	25	10	82	8	16
Edinburgh	725	50	1	50	12	60	-	50	50	5	55	333	33	48
Glasgow	1,440	109	121	159	71	53	89	21	76	46	70	815	82	96
Municipal total	**2,625**	**178**	**132**	**217**	**94**	**141**	**97**	**109**	**142**	**88**	**150**	**1,348**	**135**	**175**
David MacBrayne	135	9	14	24	6	12	16	13	5	14	8	121	12	9
GRAND TOTAL	**7,410**	**515**	**431**	**487**	**490**	**461**	**433**	**369**	**444**	**330**	**325**	**4,285**	**429**	**494**

The Albion Lowlander featured in new vehicle deliveries in the first half of the 1960s. Central SMT had ten Alexander-bodied Lowlanders, one of which is seen leaving Buchanan Street bus station in Glasgow. The raised level of the front upper deck windows accommodated the Scottish Bus Group's standard triangular destination display and provided a better view forward for the front seat passengers. New in 1963, A18 (FGM 18) operated for just two years with Central, being among the first Lowlanders to be dispatched to Highland Omnibuses in 1965.

New deliveries to major operators by vehicle type 1960–1969

Model	1960	1961	1962	1963	1964	1965	1966	1967	1968	1969	Total	Share %
DOUBLE-DECK												
AEC Regent V	7	60	22	-	-	-	-	-	-	-	89	3.5
AEC Bridgemaster/Renown	-	-	-	2	-	-	-	-	-	-	2	0.1
Albion Lowlander	-	-	19	162	7	6	-	-	-	-	194	7.5
Bristol Lodekka	85	89	106	98	103	100	65	43	-	-	689	26.8
Bristol VR	-	-	-	-	-	-	1	-	25	63	89	3.5
Daimler CVG6	19	10	8	11	8	8	-	-	-	-	64	2.5
Daimler Fleetline	-	-	-	2	20	55	60	107	60	10	314	12.2
Leyland Titan	175	153	97	-	50	-	25	-	-	-	500	19.4
Leyland Atlantean	-	-	90	70	53	88	45	136	45	107	634	24.6
Total double-deck	**286**	**312**	**342**	**345**	**241**	**257**	**196**	**286**	**130**	**180**	**2,575**	
SINGLE-DECK												
AEC Reliance	86	68	69	75	98	4	80	1	5	2	488	28.5
AEC Swift	-	-	-	-	-	-	-	-	20	15	35	2.1
Albion Viking VK43	-	-	-	-	-	49	24	74	42	34	223	13.0
Bedford C5/VAS/SB	11	8	50	28	26	19	13	4	20	6	185	10.8
Bedford VAM/VAL	-	-	-	-	6	-	1	46	31	5	89	5.2
Bristol MW	13	5	7	-	-	-	-	-	-	-	25	1.5
Bristol RE	-	-	-	-	-	-	46	-	12	24	82	4.8
Ford R	-	-	-	-	-	-	2	-	6	12	20	1.2
Leyland Tiger Cub	80	31	19	21	9	-	6	6	-	-	172	10.1
Leyland Leopard	20	7	-	21	80	103	-	26	62	34	353	20.6
Leyland Panther	-	-	-	-	-	1	1	-	1	13	16	0.9
Others	19	-	-	-	1	-	-	1	1	-	22	1.3
Total single-deck	**229**	**119**	**145**	**145**	**220**	**176**	**173**	**158**	**200**	**145**	**1,710**	
GRAND TOTAL	**515**	**431**	**487**	**490**	**461**	**433**	**369**	**444**	**330**	**325**	**4,285**	

Top five 1960s double-deck, major operators

1	Bristol Lodekka	689
2	Leyland Atlantean	634
3	Leyland Titan	500
4	Daimler Fleetline	314
5	Albion Lowlander	194

Top five 1960s single-deck, major operators

1	AEC Reliance	488
2	Leyland Leopard	353
3	Albion Viking VK43	223
4	Leyland Tiger Cub	172
5	Bedford VAS	125

Top five 1960s chassis suppliers, major operators

1	Leyland	1,675
2	Bristol	885
3	AEC	614
4	Albion	427
5	Daimler	378

Major operators' fleets, March 1966

Make/model	Alexander Fife	Alexander Midland	Alexander Northern	Central SMT	Highland	Scottish Omnibuses	Western SMT	Total
DOUBLE-DECK								
AEC Regent III	-	20	2	-	-	71	-	93
AEC Regent V	-	-	-	-	-	2	-	2
AEC Bridgemaster	-	-	-	-	-	2	-	2
AEC Renown	-	-	-	-	-	1	-	1
Albion Lowlander	25	44	2	-	12	-	111	194
Bristol Lodekka	127	114	-	290	12	219	235	997
Daimler Fleetline	-	-	-	-	-	2	54	56
Guy Arab	64	-	-	17	14	-	54	149
Leyland Titan	26	181	75	277	-	59	351	969
Leyland Atlantean	-	-	-	2	-	-	-	2
Total double-deck	242	359	79	586	38	356	805	2,465
SINGLE-DECK								
AEC Regal	-	-	35	-	-	6	-	41
AEC Regal III	-	-	6	-	4	17	-	27
AEC Regal IV	-	-	-	-	-	49	-	49
AEC Monocoach	-	35	13	-	6	97	-	151
AEC Reliance	45	63	158	-	33	264	-	563
Albion Victor	-	-	-	-	2	-	-	2
Albion Nimbus	-	13	-	-	6	-	-	19
Albion Aberdonian	5	1	20	-	-	-	-	26
Albion Viking	11	10	15	-	-	12	-	48
BMC J2	-	-	-	-	2	-	-	2
Bedford OB/A4	-	-	-	-	1	1	-	2
Bedford SB	-	9	3	20	1	1	-	34
Bedford VAS1	5	10	5	-	10	20	-	50
Bristol LS6G	20	-	-	-	-	50	19	89
Bristol MW6G	-	-	-	-	-	20	52	72
Commer Avenger	-	-	-	-	1	-	-	1
Daimler CVD6	-	-	4	-	6	-	-	10
Ford Thames 570E	-	-	-	-	7	-	-	7
Guy Arab III	45	3	-	-	7	-	-	55
Guy Arab UF/LUF	20	-	-	9	41	-	49	119
Leyland Tiger	49	100	65	-	-	1	-	215
Leyland Royal Tiger	11	57	16	-	-	4	-	88
Leyland Tiger Cub	68	207	10	-	-	4	-	289
Leyland Leopard	-	82	4	25	-	-	119	230
Land Rover	-	-	-	-	1	-	-	1
Trojan	-	-	-	-	-	1	-	1
Total single-deck	279	600	354	54	128	547	239	2,201
Total fleet	521	959	433	640	166	903	1,044	4,666

Make/model	Aberdeen	Dundee	Edinburgh	Glasgow	Total
DOUBLE-DECK					
AEC Regent III	21	59	-	126	206
AEC Regent V	30	-	-	164	194
BUT trolleybus	-	-	-	105	105
Daimler CW/CV	168	161	21	201	551
Daimler Fleetline	-	-	-	1	1
Guy Arab	-	-	130	-	130
Leyland Titan	-	-	427	465	892
Leyland Atlantean	-	-	1	313	314
Sunbeam trolleybus	-	-	-	5	5
Total double-deck	**219**	**220**	**579**	**1,380**	**2,398**
SINGLE-DECK					
AEC Regal IV	-	5	-	-	5
Albion Aberdonian	-	-	1	-	1
Bedford VAS1	-	-	4	-	4
Bedford SB5	-	-	12	-	12
Bedford VAL14	-	-	6	-	6
BUT trolleybus	-	-	-	8	8
Daimler CVD6	7	10	-	-	17
Leyland Royal Tiger	-	-	17	-	17
Leyland Olympic	-	-	1	-	1
Leyland Worldmaster	-	-	-	18	18
Leyland Tiger Cub	-	-	101	-	101
Leyland Leopard	-	-	1	-	1
Leyland Panther	-	-	-	1	1
Total single-deck	**7**	**15**	**143**	**27**	**192**
Total fleet	**226**	**235**	**722**	**1,407**	**2,590**

Source: PSV Circle publication SSA2

Albion's big home market success in the 1960s was the rear-engined Viking VK43, which was bought in large numbers by SBG. All of the SBG vehicles had Alexander Y-type bodies (some of which were built by Potters in Belfast) and most were 40-seaters. There were 48 in SBG service in March 1966, including Northern's NNV14 (DRG 954C), seen when new in the company's Rosehearty depot in the summer of 1965.

Five strong men push a broken-down Central SMT Lodekka out of Buchanan Street bus station and on to the vacant land used for bus parking, where it will be out of the way until help arrives. It's the summer of 1965, and the Lodekka is barely 12 months old. No high-visibility jackets. No anxious health and safety inspectors warning against the risk of strain when pushing an eight-ton bus. A family walking by as if men pushing a bus was an everyday occurrence. The 1960s were different times indeed.